Dust that Dreams of Glory

*Reflections on
Lent and Holy Week*

Michael Mayne

Edited, with an Introduction,
by
Joel W. Huffstetler

CANTERBURY
PRESS
Norwich

© The estate of Michael Mayne, 2017
Introduction © Joel Huffstetler, 2017

First published in 2017 by the Canterbury Press Norwich
Editorial office
3rd Floor, Invicta House
108–114 Golden Lane
London EC1Y 0TG, UK

Canterbury Press is an imprint of Hymns Ancient & Modern Ltd
(a registered charity)

Hymns Ancient & Modern® is a registered trademark of
Hymns Ancient & Modern Ltd
13A Hellesdon Park Road, Norwich
Norfolk NR6 5DR, UK

www.canterburypress.co.uk

British Library Cataloguing in Publication data

A catalogue record for this book is available
from the British Library

978 1 78622 017 2

Typeset by Manila Typesetting Company
Printed and bound in Great Britain by
CPI Group (UK) Ltd

Contents

In memory of John and Anne Maley

Foreword

BY LUCY WINKETT

Perhaps it's not surprising that the title of this book is reminiscent of the evocative line from that most humane of playwrights, Oscar Wilde. In *Lady Windermere's Fan*, he has his character reflect: 'We are all in the gutter, but some of us are looking at the stars.' Lord Darlington, the character who is given this line, is a friend of Lady Windermere, whose life is turned upside down by her own suspicions of her husband and then by her estranged mother's return.

Michael Mayne writes not only as a priest, a theologian and a spiritual guide, but as such a friend of our muddled, often contradictory humanity. That our life can be characterized as 'dust that dreams of glory' is at once both a hopeful and merciful thought that typifies his spirituality, whose own illness shaped much of his compassionate pastoral response to the many people who sought him out.

This set of reflections and sermons reveals his ability to be brave. To stay, for example, with the Devil's challenge '*If* you are the Son of God', and for that to foster an adventurous not destructive reaction to a person of faith wondering how to develop their trust in Christ. He has an admirable impatience with what he calls 'mushiness', too, while at the same time illuminating human need and frailty in a way that is kind, and that raises the possibility of healing.

His writing evokes a deep, perhaps even insatiable appetite for mystery, affirming that for him, 'not knowing' is more of a gift than a burden. And his own reflections on his suffering and incapacity when he was diagnosed with ME are poignant, as they open a window not only into the condition itself but into the ambivalence with which it was viewed by medics.

Michael Mayne writes in a way that is learned and steeped in the Christocentric theology that shaped him, but also in a way that is spacious; that allows us as readers to find our own room, stretch our own spiritual muscles and ask our own, never-too-basic questions. 'Here is a God', he reflects, 'who shares the dirt and the pain, the weakness and the loneliness, the very death that we experience ourselves.' But this God is never a desolating presence or a downbeat companion. The stars and the glory are somehow still above us, just out of reach, even when we feel ourselves to be in the dust or the gutter. Our life is held within the divine life, shot through with the hope of glory, within sight if not reach of the stars.

The Christ who accompanied Michael Mayne to his death seems to have been for him the bringer of ultimate compassion and incomparable love. The God who was preached by Michael at Westminster Abbey, and is preached by him still in these pages, is the God who says in Jesus: 'I love you because you are you.'

Acknowledgements

Thanks are due to the faculty and staff of Sarum College, Salisbury, where the majority of the selection and editing of this collection took place during a sabbatical leave in 2016. Thanks also to Martyn and Emma Percy for the hospitality extended during my stay in their home in Oxford. Much work on this project took place overlooking Alice's Garden.

Thanks to Dan and Sarah Mayne Tyndall for the lovely weekend Debbie and I enjoyed with you and the people of St Mary Redcliffe, Bristol, and for the encouragement we received toward this project.

This collection of addresses would not exist without the help and support of Alison Mayne. Thank you, Alison.

The final month of sabbatical time in 2016 was spent at the beach home of Hal and Andrea Roe, where a significant amount of editing took place among far more leisurely pursuits. Thanks, dear friends, for your gracious gift of time at the beach, and for the heads up regarding Charlene!

Christine Smith and the staff at Canterbury Press share my passion for bringing more of Michael Mayne's work to light. Thank you.

To our dear friends in St. Luke's Episcopal Church in Cleveland, Tennessee: Debbie and I will never forget your gracious gift of sabbatical time in 2016. Our love to you, always.

My wife Debbie has partnered with me at every stage in bringing this book to life. Thank you, my love, for sharing the vision, and for your belief in me which often exceeds my own.

All editor's royalties are donated to Horatio's Garden, Salisbury Hospital, in honour of Alison Mayne and in memory of Michael Mayne.

Joel W. Huffstetler
Cleveland, Tennessee

Introduction

The addresses in this collection were given by Michael Mayne from 1985 through to 1999. Many were offered in Westminster Abbey, while others were offered in churches throughout England and the United States.

Mayne's passion was to proclaim the good news of Christ in thoughtful, thought-provoking and wholly accessible language, so that the widest possible audience might receive Christ's message of the merciful, affirming and redemptive love of God. Reading through these addresses, one is struck by their timeless quality.

Michael Mayne loved a phrase from Richard Holloway (b. 1933), Bishop of Edinburgh and then Primus of the Scottish Episcopal Church: 'dust that dreams'. This new collection of Lenten addresses, *Dust that Dreams of Glory*, is representative of Mayne's tireless proclamation of Christ's love for and redemption of humanity in all our frailties. Dust yes; but we are the beloved dust of our creator whose love never ceases.

Once asked: 'What should I give up for Lent?' Mayne replied: 'Feeling guilty!' The addresses in this collection present readers with a positive vision of Jesus Christ who implores humanity to choose love over indifference, compassion over self-interest, and unity over estrangement.

Following an appearance as guest preacher at Harvard, Mayne received a letter of thanks from a Canadian woman who had been among the gathered that day in Massachusetts. In the letter she writes, 'Such fine preaching should be heard by many.' In *Dust that Dreams of Glory*, Mayne's consoling and enlivening pastoral voice lives on.

PART 1

Lent

I

A Day for Honesty
Ash Wednesday

Lord, have mercy upon me a sinner. Luke 18.13

When the Empress Zita of Austria/Hungary died aged 97, her funeral was held in St Stephen's Cathedral in Vienna. When the cortège arrived, the doors of the church were closed. The Chamberlain knocked three times with his staff and one of the friars inside called out, 'Who requests entry?'

The reply was: 'Her Majesty, Zita, Empress of Austria, Crowned Queen of Hungary, Queen of Bohemia, Dalmatia, Croatia, Slavonia and Illyria, Archduchess of Austria, Grand Duchess of Tuscany . . .' And so it went on, ending with all her orders.

The friar replied: 'We do not know her. Who requests entry?' 'Her Majesty Zita, Empress of Austria, Queen of Hungary.' Again the reply came: 'We do not know her. Who requests entry?' This time the Chamberlain replied: 'Our sister Zita, a poor, mortal sinner.' 'Let her enter!' And the doors were thrown open.

'Lord,' said the publican in the Temple, 'have mercy upon me, a sinner.'

Many churches and cathedrals are built in the shape of the cross: a cross, which is the placing together of a vertical and a horizontal shaft. The vertical speaks of God, who is both infinitely beyond us and is also the ground of our being in whom we are rooted. The horizontal speaks of neighbour, those whose lives I touch for good or ill day by day. And to stand at the centre, aware of the twin demands to love God and neighbour, is to understand how costly this can be. It means that discipline of the giving attention to God which is prayer and worship, and that giving attention to each other which passes by the name of love.

Ash Wednesday is a day for honesty: a day when we admit how far short we continually fall in trying to live at this point of intersection where our proper awareness of God meets our proper awareness of each other.

On Ash Wednesday we are invited to come to the altar rail, kneel and be signed on the forehead with the sign of the cross from the ashes of the burnt palm leaves from the last Palm Sunday, while these words are said: 'Remember that you are dust, and to dust you shall return. Turn away from sin and be faithful to Christ.' This is a very ancient custom which for a thousand years has been done in the greater part of Christendom.

If we choose to come forward for the imposition of ashes, it must be because we wish it and believe that it will speak to us on our Christian journey both of our own mortality and weakness and of the gracious love of God that time and again remakes us and affirms our value in his sight. This symbolic action can be a powerful way of committing ourselves to take Lent seriously as we each try afresh to grow in the love and knowledge of God and the service of one another.

2

Dust that Dreams of Glory

If you are the Son of God . . . Luke 4.3

Luke 4.1–13 is all about temptation: the temptations that Jesus faced in the desert. They are subtle, undermining temptations, for they go to the very heart of who he is and what he has come to do.

His temptations arise from his baptism. At the moment of his baptism he understands who he is and what his mission is to be: he is aware of God saying to him 'Thou art my son', and his mission is both to reveal God as Father and to preach the kingdom. But now in those long weeks in the desert he hears another voice. It says:

> If you are the Son of God, then how will you fulfil your vocation as God's Messiah? How will you make people listen? How will you use your very considerable powers? Surely, as the Son of God, you could perform a miracle. You could turn stones into bread and so win the gratitude of huge numbers of people. Or you could win worldly power and become a national hero by leading the zealots to armed insurrection against the Romans. Or you could test God in the most dramatic way by leaping from the pinnacle of the Temple to the valley far below, knowing God will keep you safe. And in one of these spectacular ways you could compel people to believe in you.

Now these are real temptations that come to Jesus as he wrestles in the desert with the form his ministry is to take – and he rejects them all. He knows that if he is to reveal the true nature of God then he must show that there is more to life than satisfying our physical needs. He must show that God's way is not the world's way. He must show that the way of self-giving love is always costly, and he must show that God is to be trusted, come what may, but not put to the test.

But I want to pursue what is for me a more intriguing temptation. For note the words St Luke puts in the devil's mouth. He doesn't say, '*Because* you are the Son of God you can choose to do this or that', he says '*if*' – '*If* you are the Son of God.' Jesus must confront the question: 'Who am I?' I believe wrestling with this question was the real desert experience for Jesus. Was he really the Messiah? Could he trust his deep inner conviction that through him the Father was going to be revealed in a new and unique way – and trust that conviction whatever the cost and wherever it took him?

Here is a mystery we can only ponder, yet I find it a very fruitful line of thought. Of course I am tempted – as you are – to seek to live by bread alone, simply to live for the satisfaction of my material needs. Of course I am tempted – as you are – to live by worldly standards rather than God's. Of course I am tempted – as you are – to put God to the test, to look for special protection especially when sickness or danger threatens. And it's all because I doubt that I really am a child of God. That's the real temptation: my reluctance to become what I truly am – my failure to grasp and to live by the life-changing truth that I am baptized, that I am a child of God: in St Paul's words, an 'heir of God and a joint heir with Christ'. If it is true that we are sons and daughters of God, then we must act as if we believe it.

'*If* you are the Son of God . . .' Jesus learned from his desert experience to accept both that he was the Son of God in a unique sense, and also what that meant for him in terms of faith and action – that is to say, in terms of trust and love.

'If *we* are the sons and daughters of God', then we must learn to trust and to love. It is in what we might call the desert experiences of life – in the dark times or the arid and painful times – that we are tempted to doubt or despair, tempted to forget that the Christlike God is with us at every moment of our lives, that it is in him that we live and move and have our being: that we are his children, come what may. And it is precisely in those times – in times of illness or bereavement, in times of loneliness or depression, in times when our prayer seems dead – that we need all the more to affirm: 'I am baptized. I am redeemed. I am in Christ, and he is in me. I am a child of God, made in his likeness.'

That's not to say that we look to God to give us special protection in this unpredictable world. We Christians are not exempt from the lightning flash or the cancer cell, from accident or sudden death. If we leap off pinnacles of temples we shall be killed. What it does mean is that we become those who say with Job, 'Though he slay me, yet will I trust him', or with the dying Jesus: 'Father, into your hands I commit my spirit.'

To be open to God is to achieve that kind of trust and that kind of hope, and part of that trusting and hoping lies in resisting the temptation to despair about human nature in the face of the violence, the naked aggression and the brutality that we see nightly on the news or daily in the press. To despair is to doubt God and to be blind to the countless unrecorded acts of human courage, compassion, forgiveness and healing that are occurring all around us if only we had eyes to see. Our task is to celebrate all that is clearly of God and so keep hope alive.

On Ash Wednesday some of us have ash placed on our forehead with the words: 'Remember that you are dust, and to dust you shall return. Turn away from sin and be faithful to Christ.' Yet Lent is not a bleak, forbidding time, but a very positive and optimistic remembering of who and what we truly are. 'Dust', yes, but dust that dreams of glory. Dust that has been claimed by God. Dust that has a deep, aching sense both of its mortality and of its reaching after the God glimpsed in Jesus whom one day we shall see face to face. Lent is a time for remembering where our true home lies, and for setting our face once again in that direction.

3

Terrible and Tender

Compassion and forgiveness belong to the Lord our God, though we
have rebelled against him. Daniel 9.9

At first sight, the God of the Old Testament doesn't score high
marks for consistency. Sometimes he is experienced as anger
and sometimes as love. And those who preach a God – as I've
often been tempted to – who is a kind of comforting cotton-wool
superdaddy, all-embracing and soft and mushy with no hard
edges, forget one thing: his wrath.

In Genesis 6.11–8.22 we encounter the story of how 'God
saw that the whole world was corrupt and full of violence' and
sent the flood to destroy it, yet saved a few. A primitive tale that
speaks of God's anger. And yet it contains within it the seeds of
that other, deeper truth that the Old Testament never allows us
to forget: God's love and tenderness, the fact that 'Compassion
and forgiveness belong to the Lord our God, though we have
rebelled against him.'

The wrath and the mercy. They also intermingle in the New
Testament, certainly in Jesus. Matthew 19.41–46 sees him at one
moment weeping with great tenderness over Jerusalem, and at
the next moment angrily scourging the Temple court. The version of that scene by the painter El Greco has a man tapered like
a flame, a whip in his hand and his eyes blazing with anger, the
colours strong and violent, the scene one of wild disorder, with
tables overthrown and money on the floor.

Why did he do it? What was he angry about? He was angry
about the distortion of the house of God into a place of commer-
cial exploitation. Poor people, spending the savings of a lifetime,
would come on pilgrimage to worship in Jerusalem. They needed
a clean animal for sacrifice and the traders charged an exorbitant

rate. They brought their strange, foreign money, which had to be changed into Jewish coinage. And they were shamelessly defrauded. Every Jew knew that this was a racket, but no one dared do anything about it. This is what Jesus saw in the Temple, and his hatred of injustice and his compassion for the poor and the exploited overflowed into anger.

But it is a holy anger. It isn't bad temper. It isn't the kind of anger that so often suffuses us and makes us shout and bang about. For that is usually self-indulgent and has to do with self-pity. For one thing, his anger is controlled and it is premeditated. St Mark tells us it was late afternoon when these things came to our Lord's notice, and so he comes back the next day, perhaps after gathering a group of supporters to help him. The action is planned in advance. This anger of Jesus, which reflects the wrath of God, is a righteous anger that needs to be expressed because nothing else has any chance of startling men and women into the realization of what they are doing. The motivation is not hate but love.

If as his followers we are called to see the world through the eyes of Jesus, as well as to see Jesus especially in the poor and the oppressed, then we have a duty to be angry with a holy anger that will sometimes force us to act.

Now, compassion and anger go hand in hand. What we do about it depends on us. Sometimes we feel powerless to do more than give our money or pray. But we shan't even do that much unless we see that love of God and love of neighbour are the inseparable head and tail of the coin of our faith; that, as Gandhi said, unless we see God in the very next person we meet, there is no point in looking for him further.

One of the most difficult decisions Christians face is how far anger should be translated into violence. I guess most of us would say that, in any attempt to bring about radical change, we may only resort to non-violent means, for that is to follow the way of Christ on the cross. He broke the vicious circle of violence by taking upon himself the violence of men, and then refusing to pay back violence for violence. 'You have heard it said, "An eye for an eye and a tooth for a tooth". But I say unto you, "Forgive your enemies."' The Christlike witness of a Gandhi, or a Desmond Tutu in South Africa, who believe in the power of non-violent action to bring about social change, is extremely effective. But remember: that kind of courageous witness is fuelled by a holy anger that such injustice should exist.

Like Jesus in the Temple we ought to respond to injustice, exploitation or oppression with a controlled and holy anger. For that is a reflection in us of a God who hates evil, a God who is both terrible and tender, gentle and a 'consuming fire' – a God of judgement and mercy, a God who sets his face against injustice and yet never ceases to love those who perpetrate it, and who longs for them to turn and repent.

The wrath and the mercy, the anger and the compassion – can't we see that even in ourselves they can both be an expression of our love? The fire and the rose are one.

Love is not mushy: it has this double charge – it can be gentle and it can be violent. For if we are to love good, we must hate evil. The opposite of love is not anger, it's indifference. It's that grey, detached, non-interfering keeping oneself to oneself – proud indifference. That's what almost broke Jesus' heart. Against it he used the only effective weapon, his anger, in order that they – we – may turn and repent. And if we look more deeply into that picture of a man with a whip in his hand and fire in his eyes in the Temple court, we shall understand that all that wrath is for the sake of the sinner as much as the sinned against. For in God, the language of wrath is the language of love.

4

A Gracious God, Full of Compassion

If anyone speaks against the Holy Spirit, for him there is no forgiveness, either in this age or in the age to come. Matthew 12.32

She was in her thirties and she sat with me in my study showing all the signs of acute distress. Finally, she was able to voice what was causing her so much anguish: 'I know I have committed the sin against the Holy Ghost and I can never be forgiven.' And not for the first time in my ministry I had to try, gently but firmly, to assure her she was wrong: to try to replace her groundless fear with the truth of the compassionate loving forgiveness of God as that is revealed in Jesus Christ.

And yet the words of Jesus stand: 'If anyone speaks against [in other translations, 'slanders'] the Holy Spirit, for him there is no forgiveness, either in this age or in the age to come.'

Someone once wrote a book on what are called the hard sayings of Jesus and called it *What Jesus REALLY Meant*, which is a patronizing title if ever I heard one. But the fact remains: this is a hard saying. So what does it mean and is it true?

I believe we have to ask three questions. First, can we be sure Jesus actually used those words? Second, if he did use them, what was the context in which they were said? Third, how do they fit within the whole spirit of the Christian understanding of a gracious God?

So did Jesus use the words? The answer is that we simply don't know. For consider this: Jesus was speaking in Aramaic in rural Galilee. For at least a generation the events of his life and death and resurrection, together with his sayings, stories and parables, were repeated in oral form and circulated within the local Christian churches. Eventually the evangelist wrote them down, using various sources, and he wrote them in Greek in, say, urban Antioch. Repeated church use must have distanced and adapted Jesus' words, so that it's hard to be certain of their complete authority. For example, St Luke, in telling his version of this incident, leaves out the most ominous phrase about not being forgiven 'either in this age or in the age to come' – so was it there or not?

But if Jesus did use the words, or something like them, what is their context? The answer is, a very dramatic and challenging one for Jesus. The lawyers, the experts in the law of Moses, have come down to Galilee from Jerusalem to investigate reports of Jesus' healing and exorcizing people. They accept that people are being healed but give it a sinister explanation and say that Jesus must be doing the work of Satan. The early Church saw the healing power of Jesus as the work of God: creative and loving works of mercy. The lawyers and Pharisees, by saying 'this is of the devil', by saying, 'this is black magic', are therefore not only remaining blind to the work of God but are actually opposing it, opposing the Holy Spirit, whom they saw as the one who reveals the truth of God to us and who also enables us to recognize the truth when we see or hear it.

So what Jesus is accusing them of is a wilful blindness, a deliberate inverting of the truth: calling good evil and evil good – calling light darkness, beauty ugliness and the truth a lie.

Now if that is the setting for Jesus' fierce warning, how are we to understand the words today, and indeed, how can they be made to fit into the fundamental Christian belief that Jesus did not come into the world to condemn it but to save it, and the whole Christian understanding of the gracious, loving, ever-forgiving God?

The key that unlocks the answer is to realize that this 'sin that has no forgiveness' is not a sin: it's not certain kinds of behaviour or words or actions that spoil us and for which we may ask and receive forgiveness. It is rather the condition of one who has lost the ability to distinguish between light and darkness, good and evil. 'There is but one sin,' G. K. Chesterton once wrote, 'to call the green leaf grey.' If you imprison a person long enough in the dark they will lose the ability to see. If you never got out of bed you would lose the ability to walk.

If you act totally selfishly with no thought for the effect your action is having on others, you lose the power to discriminate between right and wrong. If you have no awareness of ever needing to forgive or be forgiven, you cannot experience forgiveness. If you can no longer distinguish between good and evil then you reach the condition of effectively saying, 'Evil, be thou my good.' And then not even the Christlike God revealed in the incarnation can have any power to move your heart. Indeed, you will do all you can to crucify him.

But are we then to say that for many there can be no forgiveness, 'either in this age or in the age to come'? No – we are to make no such assumption. We are to hear the warning and leave God to do the judging. All we do know is that there is no higher gift than human freedom. That includes our freedom to call the green leaf grey, and to crucify the good and the just in every age. Whether in the end a human being can be so consumed by self, or by the doing of evil, that he or she is eventually extinguished like a candle flame without oxygen, we can't judge. That's God's business, not ours.

But what we do know is that even as they crucified Jesus he went on saying, 'Father, forgive them, for they know not what they do', and that the God in whom we believe is a gracious God, full of compassion, his judgement always matched by his mercy, who, even as we turn to meet him in penitence, comes running to meet us and welcome us home.

5

Victorious Acceptance

And being in agony he prayed more earnestly; and his sweat became like
great drops of blood . . . Luke 22.44

In 1985 a debilitating illness knocked me flat in the midst of an
extremely busy and quite stressful parish ministry. It was to pre-
vent me working for almost a year, keep me housebound for six
months, and only leave me finally some three or four years later.
Its chief symptoms, all of them lasting for more than a year, were
constantly swollen glands, pains in the chest, extreme weakness
in the muscles of the legs and arms, aching limbs, a sense of a
great weight on the lungs and a feeling of nausea, together with
a kind of dottiness so that I couldn't remember things or find the
right words. I was so diminished that it was impossible to walk
even around our small garden and difficult to climb the stairs to
bed.

I had endless tests: chest X-rays, blood tests, heart tests, hours
hanging around in those dreary hospital corridors and clinics,
and eventually I was told it was a kind of post-viral fatigue
state that should pass in a few weeks. But it didn't. It was only
in September 1986, 16 months after I was first taken ill, that
I finally saw a distinguished neurologist who said: 'You have
myalgic encephalomyelitis – in other words ME.' Myalgic refers
to the muscles; encephalo refers to the inflammation of the brain
and nervous system. Even ten years ago not much was known
about ME; much more is known about it now. The World
Health Organization now lists it as a disease of the central nervous system, and research in the past few years has proved that
it is an organic illness triggered by the entero-virus group of
viruses. It is caused by an abnormal response to a viral infection,
which results in an overactive immune system and inflammation

throughout the central nervous system, and a persistent infection of the brain stem. If you are lucky, you may recover in a year or two but many take very much longer. The illness was not helped by some of the papers labelling it 'yuppie flu', nor by the fact that some GPs are still ignorant of its causes and its nature and prove unsympathetic. Perhaps that's because, as with all illnesses, doctors have neurotic patients who will claim to be victims of whatever disease is fashionable at the time. But believe me, ME is very real and very unpleasant, and those who have the genuine thing deserve a lot of sympathy.

I don't want to bore you with details of my illness and slow recovery, but I do want to share with you some of the things I learned from that experience.

I learned what it feels like when your life is suddenly and gravely diminished, for then the whole of you is diminished – body, mind and spirit – especially if you have an illness that is not diagnosed or defined. When your life grinds to a halt, all that motivates you is called in question, and you are at once wholly dependent on the professional skill of doctors. And you feel anxious, even guilty. 'What is wrong with me?' 'Will I get better?' 'How long will it take?' 'Are the doctors telling me the truth?' 'What about my work?' 'Have I in some way, by stress or overwork, brought this on myself?' And in the case of a life-threatening illness, 'Why me?' And if the illness persists, 'Why does God appear to be so silent, so resistant to my prayers?' There may also be a great sense of isolation, for however close you are to your wife or husband or some close friend, and though they may be a model of supportive and affirming care, ultimately we face our illness, as we face our death and our dying, alone.

You need above all to be listened to for the person you are. For the first few weeks I felt I was treated by the doctors as no more than a collection of interesting symptoms. Only when I discovered a marvellous old homeopathic, holistic doctor did I feel I was given proper attention. He said: 'Tell me about yourself: tell me how you feel. Tell me about your life and your work.' He talked about my breathing, my posture, my diet. And he listened. And that was important because a patient experiences illness as the disruption, even the possible disintegration of their ordinary lives, and seeks someone who will share the journey with them, not just someone who has the expertise to analyse X-rays. In Solzhenitsyn's novel *Cancer Ward*, one of the characters complains to Dontsova, the doctor:

> You see, you start from a completely false position. No sooner does a patient come to you than you begin to do all his thinking for him. After that, the thinking's done by your standing orders, your five-minute conferences, your programme, your plan and the honour of your medical department. And once again I become a grain of sand, just like I was in the prison camp. Once again nothing depends on me.

It's very easy for professional people, especially priests and doctors, to hide behind our professional status, partly because we haven't enough time, partly to protect ourselves. We hide behind our religious jargon or our medical jargon, and often at some cost to those who look to us for help. Dame Cicely Saunders, founder of St Christopher's Hospice, writes:

> I once asked a man who knew he was dying what he needed above all in those who were caring for him. He said, 'For someone to look as if they are trying to understand me.' Indeed, it is impossible to understand fully another person, but I never forget that he did not ask for success, only that someone should care enough to try.

For quite a while in my illness I found it virtually impossible to pray. The most I could manage on good days was the saying of a psalm and reading a short passage from the New Testament. The psalms are remarkable: they really do express every kind of emotion from total trust and confidence in God to extreme anger, desolation and despair. And what I discovered during those really bad weeks was that it didn't matter that I couldn't pray, because as part of the local body of Christ I was being prayed for, upheld and supported by other members of the community. I had to learn that most difficult of lessons: what it means to receive and be served by others, rather than doing all the running myself.

When I did pray, it was to ask that most obvious of things: that I should get better, made well and active again. And it didn't seem to happen. Then one day I was visited by a remarkable nun, who put to me a very simple and obvious question but one I hadn't considered. 'You should ask yourself', she said: 'What do I really want? What, in the deepest place of myself, do I most desire?' And when I began to think about that question, especially with regard to my relationship with God, I came up with a different answer. For I knew that what I really wanted was for this whole experience of illness somehow to be redeemed, for good to come out of it. And I knew that this is always the right question to ask, for there are many conditions for which there will be no physical cure. Of course it's natural to ask for healing, and to pray for the healing of others, but that healing may be in terms of a healing of the spirit, a wholeness of the personality, of growth in trust or compassion, and not necessarily a healing of the physical body. Prayer is about attuning yourself to the love of God, who wills all that is good for us, but it doesn't override the progress of the cancer cell or the genetic defect.

After all, our faith is centred on one who died in agony in his early thirties. In the garden of Gethsemane, Jesus prayed that he would not have to go through with the crucifixion, and he prayed until his sweat became like drops of blood; but he didn't get the answer he sought. And in Gethsemane his prayer took three forms: the first was that of pleading, the second of resignation, the third of victorious acceptance.

Jesus did not offer people perfect health and a painless death. Human bodies and minds are fragile and vulnerable. What he offers is a relationship with God of such quality that nothing can destroy it. And it is that kind of confidence and trust in God, come what may, that is the true healing of the human spirit. But it may be the way of the cross, and when Jesus appeared among them after his resurrection he still bore the marks of the nails and spear in his hands and side.

So what the cross says to Christians is that there is no experience out of which good may not be brought. In the way Christ faced his own dying, and forgave those who were destroying him, we discover that there is no experience that may not be redeemed – no evil out of which God cannot bring good. Life is not fair: it often claims the good and the innocent as its victims. But life is about making certain choices when you find yourself the victim of sickness or pain or grief, choosing to find a way of facing what is negative and destructive in such a manner as to redeem it. We must be wary, as T. S. Eliot noted, of having the experience but missing its meaning.

Well, I was one of the lucky ones. In time I recovered. And I wrote a book about it, describing the illness but also trying to explain why in retrospect it seemed such a valuable part of my own journey.

In reflecting on the illness, I now know a little of what it feels like to live in the shadow-land with those whose lives are diminished, and in the end I am glad to have done so.

And I'm glad to have done so because I believe my sickness taught me, in the words of my old holistic doctor, how better 'to match my inscape (my inner life) with my landscape (my outer life)', to take time to be still and to wonder at things, and to be more understanding of, and I would hope compassionate towards, those who do go through a period of darkness. And to my astonishment that slim book I wrote is still in print, and it has brought me literally thousands of letters from people who have found it has helped to authenticate their own times of darkness. That, in a sense, has been the most rewarding thing of all and affirms my belief that no experience is ever wasted, provided we shed our natural shyness and share some of our common human experiences of joy and grief, of pleasure and pain a little more freely, helping each other to find meaning in the mysteries that surround us all.

6

A Hunger for Fulfilment
Feast of the Annunciation

I will praise thee; for I am fearfully and wonderfully made . . .
Psalm 139.14

Each human being is a uniquely embodied spirit. What do I mean by an 'embodied spirit'? I mean that I don't just have a body and a brain with their astonishingly complex balance of cells and nerves and muscles. I mean I am a body, a person, a self-conscious being, as the psalmist says, 'fearfully and wonderfully made'. I mean I am a creative, imaginative, questioning entity, able to laugh at myself and to empathize with the mystery that is you: able to speculate, to love and to be loved – capable of moments when I am made aware of a transcendent 'otherness' in myself, in other people and in the world about me, so that I am (however briefly) taken out of myself, and lose myself in wonder.

Moreover there is what I would call a 'God-dimension' in my life. I can give my attention equally to what lies outside me and what lies within me. And there lies within me what I can only describe as a kind of yearning, a hunger, a sense of incompleteness, a reaching out beyond myself, and a deep need to know myself loved and accepted and valued.

It is essential for us to recognize what a vital part music can play in the calming and healing of the human spirit. When the cellist Pablo Casals was 93 he wrote this:

For the past eighty years I have started each day in the same manner. I go to the piano, and I play two preludes and fugues of Bach. I cannot think of doing otherwise. It is a sort of benediction on the house. But that is not its only meaning for me. It is a rediscovery of the world of which I have the joy of being a part. It fills me with awareness of the wonder of life, with a feeling of the incredible marvel of being human.

But we shouldn't just marvel that we are human. We should marvel too that we are unique. When I am fulfilled and happy I am not just a fulfilled human being, I am being my own unique self in the fullest possible way. If I have an illness I am not a case of chickenpox or carcinoma: this is *my* illness and mine alone, and wise medicine will, in its treatment, its drugs and its counselling, address me in all my *me*-ness. God's gift to each of us is our rich and distinctive individuality, and what should matter to every teacher and every doctor or counsellor is how each person's uniqueness is both recognized, drawn out and celebrated.

But let me come back to what I've called the God-dimension, this hunger of the spirit. We may experience it as a hunger for love, for beauty, for music or for art. It is, in short, a hunger for fulfilment, and I can only account for this dimension in myself if I go on to say that I am created by a God whose desire it is that I should respond to him, respond sometimes in sorrow and penitence, but always with thanksgiving and always with love.

What sort of God is this? In one sense he is an unknowable, incomprehensible God. The Jewish writer Isaac Bashevis Singer hit upon this delightful metaphor for our place in God's universe:

> It is as if you were to ask a bookworm crawling inside a copy of *War and Peace* whether it is a good novel or a bad one. He is sitting on one little letter trying to get some nourishment. How can he be a critic of Tolstoy?

But Christians believe that God is not quite unknowable, that once he spoke through Mary in the only terms we can understand: in human terms, God with us, the Word made flesh, God incarnate in our midst. And our minds must somehow hold in tension the ultimate mystery of the invisible, transcendent God who in Jesus is revealed as the Christlike God, the God who in Christ enters into all our pain and suffering and is with us equally in our times of darkness as well as in our times of light.

Like any priest, I have spent hour upon hour encouraging the unloved and listening to the wounded and the lonely. I have also known the dereliction of a long, debilitating illness, when it was almost impossible to pray at all. And all I know is that, for me, the only words that have helped have had to do with Christ crucified or, if you prefer, the Easter Christ who still bears in his hands the marks of the nails and the wound in his side. The only words that I sense have helped others have had to do with the concept of the suffering God, whose love for each of us cannot be altered or diminished, and of whom I can say with the psalmist: 'If I reach up to heaven thou art there: if I go down to hell thou art there also.'

Many people come to church seeking healing in the deepest, spiritual sense, and that healing will have much to do with being affirmed and valued, being noticed and taken seriously and shown that they matter. Too many people have never been hugged. There is no substitute for the healing force of loving and being loved. I know, from my own experience, how isolated the sick can begin to feel: how cut-off, even from God, and how deep the need may be of an affirming touch and the assurance of their continuing worth. It's a very striking aspect of the ministry of Jesus that he noticed and affirmed individuals – the blind, the guilty and the diseased, as well as social outcasts like Zacchaeus, Mary Magdalene and Levi. And the fact that he stops and gives them his full attention is the beginning of their healing.

So then, perhaps the most fundamental truth of all that our churches need to express is that you, whoever you are, have worth, and if human worth, then eternal worth. Acceptance means being noticed, and because it reaches to our deepest need it is a valuable part of healing. It is not just the human lover who affirms the value of the one he or she loves with the words, 'I love you because you are you.' It is God who in Christ says those words to each one of us. But the only way he can say it now is literally through people like us.

7

The Healing Power of Forgiveness

Promise that these two sons of mine may sit one at your right hand and the other at your left in your kingdom. Matthew 20.21

The mother of James and John, Jesus' disciples, only figures in the Gospels twice. Matthew, Mark and John tell us that she was among the women who were at the cross when Jesus was crucified, and John tells us that she was the sister of Jesus' mother, Mary, which makes James and John his first cousins. Her second appearance is to plead the cause of her two sons when Jesus is on his final journey to Jerusalem for the Passover. She comes to ask that they may sit in the two places of honour in Jesus' promised kingdom. She pushes forward, kneels in Jesus' path and asks this special favour: 'Promise that these two sons of mine may sit one at your right hand and the other at your left in your kingdom.'

This is, in fact, a story about ambition – the ambition of James and John who, to the resentment of the other disciples, stake their claim for a position of prominence and power, and who do so through their mother. For fuelling and nurturing their own ambition would seem to be their mother's ambition for them. And hers is an ambition born of love – or is it?

In recent weeks I have been seeking to counsel a middle-aged man whose mother has died recently. All his life he felt he was a disappointment to her. She wanted him to be an achiever – a success in his (but more often her) chosen fields. But he never matched her expectations. He could never come up with the goods. And now with her death he is experiencing sharply and destructively the guilt and anger he was never able to express in her lifetime: all the love, but all the resentment too.

I have no doubt that if you had questioned her about her ambition for her son – that he might be successful as the world judges success – she would have replied it was because she loved him. And because the relationship of parent and child is at once the most complex, the most rewarding and the most potentially disastrous of all our relationships, many of us spend our lives either trying to get it right or learning how to put it right when it goes wrong. There is only one way to do that: through the healing power of forgiveness. And even after death, as my bereaved friend still has to discover, there can be a healing of memories and a forgiveness that will eventually set him free of her demanding spirit.

Now because part of each of us is always the child of our parents, and because some of us are also parents of our own children, we can each catch the echoes of that request from the rather pushy mother of James and John, and scent the danger of ambition masquerading as love.

It was a wrong request on two counts. First, she was ambitious – as her sons were – for the wrong things. 'Isn't it astonishing?' St Matthew is asking us by recording the incident. Even as the end draws near, with the cross already casting its long shadow and the air heavy with the sense of darkness, the mother of James and John, apparently with their connivance, is still thinking as the world thinks. And Jesus says:

But I'm offering a cup of suffering. I'm offering brokenness on a cross. I'm offering my followers a struggle whereby trust and hope are maintained, perhaps through long years of darkness, illness, doubt, and grief. Is your ambition to share the joy of Easter? Then you must first face the darkness of the cross.

Are they ambitious for power and true authority? Then they must open their eyes to the God revealed in the one who chooses to be powerless, to take a towel and wash his people's feet and so reveal the meaning of that self-giving love which is at the very heart of creation.

But the mother of James and John is not only ambitious for the wrong things. She is ambitious out of a mistaken concept of what love requires of her. It isn't wrong for a mother to be ambitious for her child – but only if she is ambitious for her child to be set free and to become a whole and integrated human being. Only love that is a giving away, a giving of yourself for the sake of another, is that love which is of God.

To be ambitious for your child is to long for that response of love that comes from one who knows himself to be his or her own person, gladly and lovingly set free, in the words of Cecil Day-Lewis, 'like a winged seed loosed from its parent stem'.

Yet perhaps we shouldn't judge too harshly one who had not yet learned that lesson and who may be unfairly treated by preachers wanting to make a point. For Mark – who wrote the earlier Gospel – has the sons of Zebedee themselves asking for the places of honour. Only Matthew chooses to let their mother take the blame, as mothers, down the centuries, have been content to do.

But she serves us well if she reminds us that there is only one kind of ambition that does not conflict with love, and that is God's ambition in creating us. And his ambition for us knows no bounds. He made us from dust, and in his love he gave us freedom; but he made us to dream of glory. Alone in all creation we can see both what is and what might be. Jesus is what might be: what we might be, and one day – by God's grace, as members of the body of Christ – will be. In the words of St Irenaeus, inscribed on the grave of Archbishop Michael Ramsey, 'The glory of God is a living man, and the life of man consists of beholding God.'

It is God who has made you your own unique, open and unfinished self, made by Love for love. It is God who says in Jesus, 'I love you because you are you.' That is your mystery and mine, as it is our ambition and our hope that one day we shall no longer see in riddles or stumble in the dark, but see God in all his beauty.

8

To Console and to Enliven
Passion Sunday

And God will wipe away all tears from their eyes . . . Revelation 21.4

The passion of Jesus is anything but passive. It was not imposed on him, nor did he passively accept it. He chose it; and he chose it because there was no other way he could act if his life was to remain consistent, and then he used it creatively. He had said to his disciples words that must have stopped them in their tracks: 'If you would be a follower of mine, take up your cross and follow me.'

For many of those who first heard those words, following Christ was to mean persecution and martyrdom – in some cases, quite literally, a cross. And still today, if you live in certain parts of the world, open criticism of an evil government that stems from what you believe about God or about the sanctity of human life may mean persecution, house arrest or summary execution.

But taking up the cross may also mean, as it did for Jesus, learning how to meet those potentially destructive experiences – suffering, abuse or deliberate evil – in a creative and trusting, even a forgiving spirit, and so transform them. So today, acting in the spirit of Christ crucified may mean the forgiving of one who has deeply wronged you. I think of many individuals, both Protestant and Catholic, who have been the victims of terrorists in Northern Ireland and still found it possible to respond not with bitterness but with a costly, crucifying forgiveness. Again, following Christ, the readiness to spend and be spent in the service of others may mean a loss of freedom. I think of the 'foolish', heart-warming courage of Terry Waite.

What I am claiming is that there is a suffering – not of illness or accident about which we have no choice – but a willingly chosen suffering such as that of Jesus, and that is the suffering of the martyrs.

Why was Jesus crucified? Because he accepted at his baptism his vocation to be totally open to God, to show God's undiscriminating love for people of every kind, good and bad alike, to forgive hurts and offences, to eat with those considered outcasts: to challenge established values and views where they denied or obscured the values of God's kingdom and the worth of every person. And many hated him for it as, perversely, the good, the generous and the vulnerable will always be hated by that within us which feels threatened: which finds it easier to settle for the easy option, to protect our rights and interests and not to go the second mile. Jesus came to be the love of God: love that is not an easy emotion but nothing less than a deliberate and costly giving of yourself for the good of another – giving your time, your attention, if need be your very life itself.

The first potent truth to be learned, then, from the Passion of Jesus has to do with a ready acceptance of suffering, because that is the nature of any genuine and consistent love.

The second truth leads us into an even deeper mystery, which has to do with that kind of suffering we may not seek or choose.

In the face of sickness, pain and ultimately death we may ask why God did not make a different sort of world. We shall get no answer. We may go on to ask if God does not care, if he is indifferent to human pain and to the cost to human lives of containing evil. God does not answer that question, but in Jesus enters into the very heart of it. In Jesus, so we believe, God himself, the involved, incarnate God, is identified with us in all our suffering, and knows from the inside what it feels like to be its victim.

And here I come finally to my text from that passage in the book of Revelation: 'And God will wipe away all tears from their eyes.' The word 'passion', from the Latin *passio*, 'I suffer', has the same roots as that other, similar word, 'compassion', from *cumpassio*, to suffer with, to suffer alongside. And there is no way we can make sense of the Passion of Jesus unless we understand it as the compassion of God.

Human compassion, that most lovely of qualities, is the ability so to put yourself in someone else's place that you know a little what it must be like to go through their experience of suffering – and so love is drawn out of you. And in the compassion of a friend, a neighbour, a bereavement counsellor, it becomes a little easier to bear. Now what Passiontide does – what Good Friday does – is to invite us to open ourselves to the compassion of God. Not his anger but his compassion: a God who from the cross begs us to be forgiven and to know ourselves accepted, valued and loved – and then, in our turn, to be compassionate to others and share something of the costliness of the cross.

I have sometimes tried to sum up why I am a Christian by saying that it is because I believe in the Passion of Jesus and the compassion of God and that they alone make sense of life in this world – a world that has pain and suffering deeply ingrained within it, a God whom I learn from the New Testament loves me beyond my imagining, and a bringing of the two together at a place called Calvary, where I can see plain what that suffering alongside us that is compassion really means and glimpse the mystery of the open-hearted, consoling love of God.

The Passion and cross of Jesus are not some momentary blip, some fault in the central system where everything suddenly went wrong, but the single still 'frame', as it were, that reveals how God is and always will be. There can be no more consoling truth than that, nor one that touches our human experience at a deeper level.

Martin Luther observed, 'Christ's proper work is to declare the grace of God, to console and to enliven.' For ultimately, in all the glory of heaven, in the presence of all the saints and martyrs and the whole people of God, God will be seen to be what in Jesus he is declared to be: the one who by suffering alongside us reveals his Passion and his compassion, and will at the end wipe away all tears from our eyes.

9

A Radical New Understanding of God
Maundy Thursday

We love, because he first loved us. 1 John 4.19

'You call me Lord . . . that is why I wash your feet.' His action bewilders them, and Peter cries out, 'Not mine, Lord, not mine!'

Here is paradox indeed, and which of us is not bewildered by it? There is the paradox of the Maundy Thursday liturgy, placed at the critical point of Holy Week, in which we journey from a joyful eucharistic celebration into the darkness of the betrayal and arrest in Gethsemane. There is the paradox of the one whom Christians look upon as the human face of almighty God kneeling to wash his disciples' feet. There is the paradox of the unimaginable majesty of God matched only by the force of his awesome love, the traditional concept of power and authority turned on its head and redefined as loving, humble service.

We need to come to the events of Holy Week with the clear, unclouded eyes of an artist or a child. For while the events of Holy Week speak of profound mysteries that have filled the world's libraries with theological speculation, they also declare utterly simple truths that speak to the heart: the kind of truth I may hear a thousand times, and yet a truth that does not become mine until I can feel it on my pulse and know it in my heart, so that I can say: '*Now* I see, *now* I understand – and the knowledge changes me.'

I suppose that if you had asked St John why his Gospel is so different from those of Matthew, Mark and Luke – why, for example, he chooses to leave out any description of the Last Supper and replace it with the story of Jesus washing his disciples' feet – he might have said: 'Because *my* purpose is to offer a profound reflection on the nature of love and, in particular, what it means to be loved by God.' And this entails a startling redefinition of what we mean when we speak of God's glory: 'we saw his glory', writes John, in the Word made flesh, and it is 'full of grace and truth'.

That other John, the Baptist, when he wanted to contrast the power and glory of God's Messiah with his own unworthiness, could think of no more striking analogy than to say that he, John, was not worthy to unloose the straps of Jesus' sandals. Yet here, in the upper room on the first Maundy Thursday, Jesus turns all acknowledged religious and social protocol on its head by stooping and kneeling on the dusty floor in order to undo the straps of his friends' sandals and begin washing their dusty feet.

What Jesus is doing is the most menial service performed by a slave, one who had no status and no rights. In this moment and what it contains the word 'glory' is new-minted, and we see that there is a glory in the loving service of your neighbour. Here is one of those defining moments when we are invited to understand that in Jesus the majesty and loving-kindness of God are most wonderfully combined. There can be no more striking definition of what loving your neighbour actually means, nor a more dramatic encapsulation of a radical new understanding of God, than in their Lord and master kneeling at their feet on the night of his arrest.

Peter is not called on to wash the feet of others – not at that stage – but to let his Lord wash his feet. And he vigorously protests: '*You*, washing *my* feet? Never!' Those are the words of a man who suddenly finds all his familiar assumptions overturned, yet who in the next moment knows he must give in – or turn away. Peter yielded and stayed: it was Judas who left.

In churches the world over the foot-washing takes place on Maundy Thursday, symbolically acted out. But to see this action simply as an injunction to love one another in acts of caring service may be to miss the deeper truth. For, complex creatures that we are, our motives are often questionable and such service can be a subtly disguised form of pride. And the origin, the pattern and the constant motivation of our Christian journey has to be our willingness not simply to give but first to receive.

'We love,' writes St John (that is to say, 'We are only capable to love'), 'because he first loved us.' For three years Jesus has demonstrated to all who cross his path that each is loved by their heavenly Father, and within a few hours they will witness the final terrible proof of this. So now, only after he has washed their feet, does Jesus say: 'Love one another as I have loved you.' And another way of saying that is: 'Now, having seen what you have seen, *now* go about your life as those who are loved.' I guess we believe it, this deepest truth of all, this knowledge that if each one of us is accepted, forgiven, loved and valued by our Creator then it opens our eyes to each other's worth, and sets us free to reach out to one another in service and friendship and generous-hearted love.

And yet we are only half-persuaded, and we need, over and over again, to repent of our lack of trust and our little love, and let another Holy Week speak to us afresh of the God who loves us beyond our imagining and went to such dramatic lengths to win us to himself: indeed, to take us by the hand and gently draw us home.

10

A New and Different Future
Good Friday

Father, forgive them . . . Luke 23.34

In time of great darkness, when the power of evil is let loose, there may be an act of human compassion and grace that illuminates the scene and lifts the heart. As Jesus stumbles under the weight of his cross at Calvary, a woman steps forward from the crowd and wipes his brow.

I suppose we can never know if the cruelty and violence of our time are any worse than those of any other. The story of Cain and Abel is an early entrant in the stakes of violence and sudden death, and the world has never been short of both the crucifiers and the crucified. What is new in our day is that these acts of inhumanity are brought with such shocking immediacy into the intimacy of our homes.

We can react in different ways. We can, as a form of self-protection, become desensitized, unable or unwilling to understand and cope with other people's pain. Or we can begin to be dragged down and almost overwhelmed by the very force of the evil itself. Or we can distance such actions from ourselves, and see them as done by 'them', the others, the enemy, the sick or the deranged – failing to understand that the seeds of violence, retribution and revenge, the seeds of self-protectiveness and the natural desire to retaliate, are deep within our own hearts and often dictate our own actions.

But Good Friday is not a day for pretence, evasion or succumbing to the force of evil. However we may distance it, however we may package it in the fine words of the King James Bible or sweeten it with the music of Victoria (the sixteenth-century

Spanish composer), the fact remains that on Good Friday we recall a scene of the torture and slow, agonizing death of Jesus, the Son of Mary and the Son of God. But this is not just a story in the past. The passion of Jesus Christ is the story of what is happening now, in a thousand places. Timothy Rees, Bishop of Llandaff from 1931 to 1939, wrote: 'Wherever love is outraged, wherever hope is killed, where man still wrongs his fellow man, thy Passion is fulfilled.' And Good Friday stands to persuade us that God is a God who would enter our darkness and our sinfulness, our hatred and our suspicion, but not be overcome by them.

For let us not plead innocence of this world of ours and how it works; even now, at this very moment, some innocent man or woman is being battered, tortured or killed in some police cell or barrack room somewhere in the world for no other reason than that he or she is at their mercy. The Passion of Jesus, the suffering of God, goes on, and we dare not plead that we are ignorant or without blame. For the cross shows us most vividly our own alienation from God, our worldliness, our denials of Christ, our disloyalty to our friends, our selfishness. 'If we say we have no sin,' writes St John, 'we are deceiving ourselves and refusing to admit the truth.'

Let us then on Good Friday face the truth. We know all too well the realities of evil in its many forms. Yet there are those moments of grace and redemption. All the evil in the world cannot in the end destroy the spirit of love: and the events of Good Friday stand for ever to prove it. Forgiveness is at once the most costly and the most powerful weapon in the world. And it is costly because it begins for each one of us at the foot of the cross.

For consider the scene at Calvary: Jesus is being nailed to the cross. He had taught his followers what it means to live the life of the kingdom of God. He had taught his followers to forgive each other and to forgive their enemies as the only possible way to redeem the past and think creatively about the future. Now, as the nails are driven home, at the moment when the greatest wrong is done to him, he says: 'Father, forgive them.' He asks for more than a negative kind of pity. He asks that they be forgiven. And when we come to that level, we are talking about something beyond mere understanding. Things are done that cannot be undone. Jesus was put to death. Millions did die in gas chambers. And it is not enough simply to pity ignorant men and women caught up by their obedience to something so much greater than they understand. What is needed is to bring something quite new out of the cruelty and the wrong. And when Jesus prays for forgiveness, he does not pray that somehow the cross may be forgotten, erased, but that out of the cross may come a new hope and a new life for those who would have it so. What Jesus does is to look to the future, and with these words he absolves his followers from any obligation they might have felt to avenge him: the old days of 'an eye for an eye and a tooth for a tooth' are past. He has met his enemies head on. Here good is face to face with evil, and he makes plain by what principles his followers are to act in the future.

The awful thing about our desire to be avenged, to retaliate, to hit back is that it always has the effect of adding just a little more poison to the system. Forgiveness breaks the pattern, and in this way the power of sin to infect us is neutralized and something quite new is created.

When we look at the cross and hear these words of Jesus about forgiveness, we are meant to say two things: first: 'Look – that is what we can do to each other. We can hate and revile and torture and crucify each other. When attacked we can retaliate. When offended we can give offence. When hurt we can lash out.' But second: 'That is not the way of Jesus whom we follow, it is the way of the world to which, St Paul tells us, we are not to be conformed.'

So what is this alternative way?

There is a book of Laurens van der Post called *The Night of the New Moon*. In it he reflects on his experience as a prisoner of war and on the untold cruelties done by the Japanese to the British prisoners, and the effect these had on them. He writes this:

It was amazing how often and how many of my men would confess to me, after some Japanese excess worse than usual, that for the first time in their lives they had realized the truth, and the dynamic liberating power, of Jesus' words on the cross: 'Father, forgive them, for they know not what they do.' The tables of the spirit would be strangely and promptly turned, and we would find ourselves without self-pity of any kind, feeling deeply sorry for the Japanese as if we were the free men and they were the prisoners . . .

Some of you may be reminded of that other wartime story of Bishop Leonard Wilson, then the Bishop of Singapore, who was captured and tortured, and of how he constantly prayed the words of Jesus: 'Father, forgive them, for they know not what they do', and of the effect this had on those who were torturing him. One of them at the end of the war became a Christian and was baptized and confirmed by the man he had tortured.

To forgive is not to forget. We do not heal the damage we do to one another by simply pretending the past did not happen or the offence has not been committed. Those who are best at forgiving are those who do remember and do suffer, because they know how much forgiveness is going to cost them. Forgiveness isn't concerned with covering up the past: it is concerned with facing the past in such a creative way as to make possible a new and different future. It is concerned with that most basic of Christian truths, illustrated so dramatically in the events of Good Friday and Easter Day, that there is nothing that can happen to us, no evil so great, that good cannot be brought out of it – that it cannot in some way to redeemed.

It is because Jesus said 'Father, forgive them' at his moment of greatest agony that the new life of the resurrection, the new creation, the new life of the kingdom, the way of Christ is made possible. And when he appeared again in the midst of his disciples in the upper room, Jesus – having forgiven Peter his denial – told his disciples that they are now those who must forgive people their sins.

All our arguments about who did what, whose fault it was, who dominated whom are never-ending and deeply destructive. Forgiveness, on the other hand, is the reckless, joyful, God-inspired stroke of genius that brings new life both to the one who is forgiven and the one who forgives. Not until we know ourselves forgiven, and begin to practise that kind of forgiveness in our own lives, do we begin to share in Christ's risen life.

You can meditate for a lifetime on the events of Good Friday and the meaning of the cross. It speaks many truths. But nothing it says is more profound than the knowledge I now have of God's invincible love for me and forgiveness of me as I see it and know it in Jesus Christ. In the words of Dame Julian of Norwich:

Would you know your Lord's meaning? Love was his meaning. Who showed it to you? Love. What did he show you? Love. Why did he show you? For love. Hold fast to this, and you shall learn and know more about love, but you will never need to know or understand about anything else for ever and ever.

What Austin Farrer says in his book *Said or Sung* are fine and true words, and they apply to every living human being made in God's image – however damaged and disfigured that image may be – and to the way of life to which we are committed.

God forgives me with a compassion of his eyes, but my back is turned to him. I have been told that he forgives me, but I will not turn and have the forgiveness, not though I feel the eyes on my back. God forgives me, for he takes my head between his hands and turns my face to his to make me smile at him. And though I struggle and hurt those hands, for they are human, though divine – human and scarred with nails – though I hurt them, they do not let go until he has smiled me into smiling; and that is the forgiveness of God.

The Supreme Paradox
Good Friday

Yes! It is accomplished! John 19.30

Words are easily said, and usually they cost us little: conventional noises, many of them, like 'Hello', 'Goodbye', 'What a lovely day!' and 'Where are you going for your holidays?' They cost us little and they ease our way through life.

But there are times when words are costly. A letter of condolence to one who is bereaved may take a long time to compose. A poet will choose words like jewels and polish and repolish them to express exactly *this* experience and not another.

And there are times, too, when words are so significant that they carry a lasting memory: of a hurt that grows out of all proportion, or of words said in anger, maybe, or of words that comfort and heal.

It was the English bishop Lancelot Andrewes who said of the miracle of the baby born at Christmas who was the Word made flesh: 'He was the Word, yet could not speak a word.' But now that Word is crucified: Jesus, whose overriding desire has been to make the Father known as only the Son knows him; Jesus, whose words and actions have revealed the true nature of God; Jesus, the Word of God, whose words have consoled and challenged in equal measure, is now – so they think – to be silenced for ever. There are to be no more words.

We know they were wrong. There are the words of the risen Christ. And yet it is good and right for us on Good Friday to try to understand a little better what it means to hear again those extraordinary last words from the cross, recorded by the four Gospel writers. For these words are timeless words, revealing eternal truths about the God we worship and his revelation of himself in Jesus Christ. They resonate down the centuries and have spoken to every generation afresh of both the suffering and the glory of the one crucified on this day.

Each Gospel writer gives us certain of those last words of Jesus: put them together and there are seven. There is a word of forgiveness, a word of compassion, a word of dutiful love, a word of desolation, a word of human need, a word of victorious achievement and a word of trust. And the more you look at each of these words on the cross, the more you understand that they touch on every aspect of human life and every experience we may be asked to undergo.

His first word is one of forgiveness: 'Father, forgive them for they know not what they do.' It is said as the nails are driven home, at the climax of this day and night of arrest, betrayal, torture and crucifixion. And as the Greek tense makes clear, he doesn't just say it once, he keeps on saying it: 'Father, forgive them.'

In all his teaching about the Father and our relationship with him and with each other, Jesus had spoken of forgiveness. It is at the heart of a parable like that of the prodigal son, at the heart of such actions as his refusal to condemn the woman taken in adultery, at the heart of that teaching we call the Sermon on the Mount. 'When you pray,' he had taught them, 'say forgive us our trespasses, as we forgive those who trespass against us.' Now, when every human instinct is to cry out at the wrong being done, and to tread the bitter path of revenge and retribution, he says: 'Father, forgive'. In this word is revealed the meaning of the love of God: hate him, deride him, crucify him, he cannot but be true to his own nature of forgiving love.

But there is more, because 'Whoever has seen me has seen the Father.' Jesus reasserts in his final hours what he would most have us discover about God: that at the heart of love there is forgiveness, and this is the nature of the God in whose likeness we are made, and that when we choose any other path we are distorting that likeness. 'Father, forgive them, for they know not what they do.' He pleads for them in their ignorance. Of course they know what they are doing in one sense; what they do not know, because they are so blind, is that they are damaging and twisting their true humanity by acting in this fashion. All of us are creatures made by Love for love. And when we act selfishly, violently, aggressively, lustfully, spitefully, uncharitably, we damage ourselves and we kill that which is of God within us. Good Friday is the day above every other that should bring us to our knees in penitence before that timeless cross.

The second word is one of compassion and hope. One of the two thieves turns to Jesus and says, 'Lord, remember me when you come into your kingdom.' And Jesus replies: 'Today shalt thou be with me in paradise.' Paradise, the Persian word for a garden, a place where things, and in this case people, grow. That thief had nothing perhaps but a sudden flash of recognition, what you might call a gasp of hope, that the one beside him who seemed so serene and victorious in death could not be wrong. When Jesus hears that gasp of hope he accepts him and reassures and loves him out of his God-like compassionate heart.

The third word is one of dutiful love. 'And Jesus, having loved his own, loved them unto the end.' He sees at the foot of the cross the two figures of John, the beloved disciple, and his mother Mary. She, as any mother would, has tried without success to protect him from pain and suffering, but in the end she has let him go to be true to his own vocation. In the end, love is always proved in the letting go. Now all she can do for her son is simply be there in her own private torment and grief. Grief is isolating. But when Jesus speaks it is he who ministers to her and to John, not they to him. 'Woman,' indicating John, 'behold your son.' And to John: 'Behold your mother.' And at once a new relationship is established – a new motherhood, a new sonship – to take the place of the old one being ended by death. The blood relationship dies, and a greater relationship, one freely and lovingly entered into, is born.

The fourth word is one of desolation. 'My God, my God, why hast thou forsaken me?' They are the opening words of Psalm 22, a Jewish prayer Jesus would have known almost from his mother's knee, which speaks of dereliction and despair. But it goes on to a wonderful climax that speaks of those coming afterwards who will declare God's righteousness to those who will be the inheritors of this unknown man's faithfulness.

It is not in the end a psalm of despair, and yet this word of dereliction has been faithfully recorded and understood by Christians down the centuries to confirm their belief that God in Christ has known the full awfulness of human loneliness and desolation. There is a powerful mystery here. We cannot know what it meant to Jesus to undergo this all-too-human experience of darkness and separation from God. Yet it is God he calls on still. It has been the testimony of so many who have known this sense of darkness in physical or mental or spiritual suffering, that afterwards they have come to see that even here God has been present with them, though they did not know it all the time.

There is no mystery in the fifth word from the cross: 'I thirst.' It is a commonplace human cry of physical need in the long-drawn-out torture of crucifixion. The one who spent all his life in the service of others is now served by one who lifts to his lips a sponge dipped in coarse wine.

Two words remain. And the first is a cry of achievement. Not a feeble cry of 'It's finished, it's the end, I am dying', but the most triumphant, 'Yes! It is accomplished!' That's the meaning of the Greek. Here is the supreme paradox: the one who seems power-less, led out to be executed, has been in command all the time. He chose to come to Jerusalem, he chose to accept the costly suffering in Gethsemane. He has suffered with words of forgive-ness on his lips. He has shown what it means to be fully human. He has revealed the true nature of the Father. He has rebuilt the bridge between God and man. Now he offers his life back to his Father. The work of saving mankind is complete.

The crucifixion begins and ends with the same word: Father, *Abba*. At the start, 'Father, forgive them.' Now, at the close, 'Father, into thy hands I commend my spirit.' It is perhaps the most moving and the most characteristic of all Jesus' words. For what he does is once again take some familiar words of a psalm, words every Jewish mother taught her child to say immediately before sleep, 'into thy hands I commend my spirit.' But he adds that one word he has made peculiarly his own. He adds the word '*Abba*, Father.' *Abba*, the equivalent of our more intimate word, 'Dad'.

The Gospels always use for the word 'Father', when it is on the lips of Jesus, the word both in Aramaic and in Greek: '*Abba*,

Father'. And I think there can only be one reason for this: that it was a well-known idiosyncrasy of Jesus to use, when speaking to God, this intimate word by which a Jewish child addressed his or her father, and his preference for the word *Abba* expressed a relationship of extraordinary directness and intensity.

It is the view of Jesus that everything we experience is undergirded by love. He never claimed that God would protect us from the violence of life: indeed, quite the contrary. Those who witness to what is true, good, just and honest may well be called to suffer, even to die, as Jesus was. What he did say is that, 'Not a sparrow falls to the ground without your Father knowing.' He saw every natural event as within the purpose and caring of God, and for Jesus death is included in God's fatherliness and like every other human experience is an occasion for trust.

Here, then, are the words of Jesus brought together from the four Gospel writers, touching on every aspect of human life and every experience we may have to undergo. Jesus once said: 'I, if I be lifted up, will draw all men to my self.' And I suppose men and women have been drawn to God from that day to this not by the powerful eloquence of philosophers or great preachers, but time and time again by the sight of Christ crucified and the simple preaching of the cross. Yet such is the nature of love that God respects our freedom. He invites us, he never compels.

12

A Study of Hands
Good Friday

You are mine and I love you. Look, I have engraved you on the palm
of my hands. Isaiah 49.16

'The crucified Jesus', it has been said, 'is the only accurate picture
of God the world has ever seen.' That really is the most astonishing
claim – but then of course only something extraordinary can
explain the explosive force of Christianity on the first-century
world and its power to change lives ever since. Christianity claims
that the Passion of Christ, which we commemorate on Good
Friday, is the decisive moment in human history, the moment
above all others when God himself has drawn near and made
himself known. This is the mystery of Good Friday, that here on
the cross the ultimate reality is revealed for what it is, as a love
that gives itself for our sake even unto death, and in so doing
breaks the power of sin and death to destroy us.

And that contradicts all the conventional ideas of God as
remote. The cross, called by St Paul 'an offence and a scandal',
is so because the figure of Jesus in Gethsemane, before Pilate,
then stripped and mocked and flogged and nailed to the wood,
seems not so much the revelation of God as the contradiction of
everything that has been commonly believed about him: that he
is almighty, disposing of the world as he wills, untouched by the
storms that rage on earth.

But far from being removed and untouched, the very heart of
God is revealed in this despised, rejected, suffering figure. Here
is God come among us in weakness and humility to stand with
us in his world and share its pain. Once, in a particular man, all
we need to know of God is embodied. And so, says John Austin

Baker, Bishop of Salisbury from 1982 to 1993, 'The crucified Jesus is the only accurate picture of God the world has ever seen, and the hands that hold us in existence are pierced with unimaginable nails.'

The other day I was shown a set of pictures by a Romanian Jew who spent four years in a Nazi concentration camp and survived. After the war he drew a set of Stations of the Cross – pictures of Jesus during the last hours of his Passion and death. What is unusual is that each one is simply a study of hands.

In the first, Jesus' hands are seen tied with rope as he stands before Pilate, and we see the hands of Pilate as he washes them in a basin of water. In the second, Jesus' hands lift his cross. In the third, he falls and balances himself on one hand as he raises his body from the dust.

In the fourth his mother's hands are stretched towards him, protective and compassionate, as he passes her on the road. In the next the strong hands of Simon of Cyrene ease the burden as he takes the cross on himself, and then the hands of St Veronica are seen holding out the veil with which Jesus will wipe his face.

In the seventh Station, Jesus' hand is raised in blessing over the imploring, twisting hands of the women of Jerusalem. And in the next two drawings his vulnerable hands are, first, laid on the cross, and then nailed through the wrist, the fingers splayed in pain.

Finally, the gentle hands of his followers lift his body from the cross.

The hands of Jesus were a workman's hands, which had carved wood in a carpenter's shop. They had been used to heal and comfort, to encourage and to forgive. They had been used to wash his disciples' feet. They had broken the bread at the Last Supper. Now they are stilled, wounded, paralysed by the nails that hold them to a wooden cross shaped by another carpenter.

But then Jesus (we are told by St Luke), after his terrible cry of desolation says those words from Psalm 31 that would have been taught to him as a good Jew by his mother, the verse that was to be said last thing before you fell asleep: 'Father, into thy hands I commit my spirit.' It is the simplest, most childlike form of trust.

Six hundred years ago the English saint Dame Julian of Norwich wrote of God: 'In his hands he wraps and holds us. He enfolds us for love and he will never let us go.' And if you visit her shrine in Norwich you will see there a striking wooden sculpture of a huge hand – the hand of God – gently cradling a small child in its palm.

I am reminded of a lovely phrase in Isaiah in a passage in which God is speaking to his people Israel, his own chosen people who are precious in his sight. He says of them: 'You are mine and I love you. Look, I have engraved you on the palm of my hands.'

The message of Good Friday is that, in God's book, you do not win by force, by muscle, but by love. Here on the one side we see the plotting and manipulating of Annas and Caiaphas, the might of Rome and Pilate, the cruelty of the soldiers, the mindless violence and abuse of a mob, and on the other side Christ's integrity and courage and self-sacrifice, his enduring forgiveness, his implicit trust in his Father. Our world says that the nails and the spear win. But God replies: 'You're wrong. My power is made perfect in weakness.' And so Good Friday is followed by Easter Day, the crucifixion by the resurrection.

I can remember preaching on Good Friday and someone saying to me at the door: 'Well, that was a depressing address: you certainly made us feel guilty this morning.' And that made me realize I'd failed, for Good Friday is not about feeling guilty but about feeling penitent and overwhelmingly grateful. It's about seeing the costliness of love and scenting already the victory of Easter.

For Jesus taught his disciples that the terrible death he was to die was not going to be a tragedy. It was going to be used by God as a mighty divine act to give the divine answer to the sin and suffering of the world. It was going to be something powerful and majestic. .

And so we have two accounts of the Passion that between them hold together the desolation and the glory of the cross. St Mark brings out the isolation of Jesus, his cry of despair, his total sharing of our human darkness. St John tells the same story and yet he tells it, in Archbishop Michael Ramsey's words, 'with a kind of title above it, and a title beneath it, and indeed a title wrapped all around it: and that title is the word "glory"'. This terrible death was and is Christ's glory and victory, for it was an act of total, self-giving love. And total, self-giving love is the very glory of the being of God himself. 'The crucified Jesus is the only accurate picture of God the world has ever seen, and the hands that hold us in existence are pierced with unimaginable nails.'

On Easter Day, in that upper room, it is his hands that Jesus shows to his disciples. 'Behold my hands! I am no ghost.' And in those hands there are, and always will be, the marks of the nails.

So what on Good Friday, reflecting on the Passion yet scenting the victory, should be our response? 'Weep not for me!', Jesus had said to the lamenting women as he went to the cross. He doesn't want their – or our – pity. We are not to enjoy the luxury of cheap tears or respond for an hour to the awful events of this day with a surface emotion. For what he is looking for is nothing less than a shift of focus in the deepest place of our wills and hearts – another small stage in that process we call conversion.

'Christ has now no other hands but your hands', wrote St Teresa of Avila, 'no other feet but your feet. Yours are the eyes with which he now looks out in compassion on the world.' And if I were to define a Christian in terms of hands, I would have to start with that deep act of trust we are asked to make: that, whatever life may bring, ultimately we are held in the hands – or engraved on the palm – of our Creator; that we know him also to be our loving Father through the healing, forgiving, comforting, serving, bread-breaking, wounded hands of his Son Jesus Christ, who even after his resurrection still bore in his hands the marks of the nails; and that we are now to be ourselves the hands of Christ, who in his love invites us to share in his dying on the cross and to know thereby the victory and the joy of his resurrection on Easter Day.

13

The Open-hearted Love of God
Good Friday

God shows his love for us in that while we were yet sinners Christ died for us. Romans 5.8

Here I intend to speak as simply as I can about the Passion of Christ: about why Jesus died on his cross, why he was cruci-fied. Some have thought it was because God demanded a kind of blood sacrifice, that somehow Jesus came to placate an angry God who demanded suffering before he would forgive human beings their sins. What a fearsome, pagan idea!

Jesus came to be the love of God, to embody the love of God for his creation, accepting the consequences for doing so what-ever they might be. Here is love, identifying himself with us at every point, and calling us back to himself. And what we call Christ's Passion speaks of our Lord turning to face Jerusalem and almost certain death because he now knows that the way of rejection, the way of the cross, is the only way he can continue to reveal the nature of God, and be the love of God in a life and death that are of a stunning consistency of character and intention.

Christ's Passion, his suffering, illuminates all kinds of suffer-ing. It has illuminated the world of the martyrs forced into the flames. It can illuminate the life of the cancer patient dying today. It speaks to the darkness of innocent torture victims. For the gos-pel takes human suffering of whatever kind utterly seriously. It accepts that life is often unfair, always unpredictable and some-times dangerous, and that to be human means to be unsure what each day may bring. And it says: Jesus was no exception. He had no special protection. He too lived in a dangerous world, full of blind and sinful people, with no certainty of what the future held. And for him it held a cross.

But the gospel is much more than a reassuring and consoling hand in the dark. It is not a way of claiming that even the best of men cannot escape from the pain and suffering implicit in human life. For the Passion of Jesus that lies at the heart of the gospel contains two discoveries that, once you allow them to ferment away in your mind and heart, are as powerful and as liberating as any truth can be. The first discovery is about a kind of suffering willingly entered into for the sake of love; the second is about the nature of God himself. Let me spell out what I mean by each.

The Passion of Jesus is anything but passive. It was not imposed on him: he chose it. And he chose it because there was no other way he could act if his life was to remain consistent, and then he used it creatively. He had said to his disciples words that must have stopped them in their tracks: 'If you would be a follower of mine, take up your cross and follow me.'

For many of those who first heard those words, following Christ was to mean persecution and martyrdom – in some cases, quite literally, a cross. And still today, if you live in certain parts of the world, that open criticism of evil government that stems from what you believe about God or about the sanctity of human life may mean persecution, house arrest, or summary execution.

But taking up the cross may also mean, as it did for Jesus, learning how to meet those potentially destructive experiences – suffering, abuse or deliberate evil – in a creative and trusting, even a forgiving, spirit, and so transform them. 'Father, forgive them, for they know not what they do.' So today, acting in the spirit of Christ crucified may mean the forgiving of one who has deeply wronged you.

At his baptism, Jesus accepted his vocation to be totally open to God, to show God's undiscriminating love for people of every kind, good and bad alike, to forgive hurts and offences, to eat with those considered outcasts and to challenge established values and views where they denied or obscured the values of God's kingdom and the worth of every person. And many hated him for it.

We are 'to know nothing', in St Paul's words, 'but Jesus Christ and him crucified'. To preach Christ crucified is not to say to people: 'Unless you believe or do certain things God will not love you.' It is to say that God loves and cares for us before we have done the least thing about it, simply because in Christ he accepts the world he has made and chooses to restore it – at great cost to himself – to what he had originally intended it to be. It is to speak of the open-hearted love of God that so values us as to endure the cross for us. Like the father in the story of the prodigal son, our Father runs to meet his children when they are still a long way off. 'God shows his love for us', writes St Paul, 'in that while we were yet sinners Christ died for us.'

14

Love Incarnate
Good Friday

Father, forgive . . . Luke 23.34

On Good Friday none of us need persuading that the power of evil is abroad in our world. Daily we see and hear of acts of violence and aggression, the wrong use of power, the abuse of the innocent and the neglect of the needy. And there are some acts that are so terrible and horrific that we almost despair of human nature and are lost for words. A headline in *The Independent* once read: 'May God forgive them, because we can't.'

I can think of no better text for Good Friday than that. And I suppose, in the light of such acts, only one form of prayer is valid: those words that are at the heart of the Eucharist and have been said or sung by the Church for the past 1,300 years: 'O Lamb of God, that takest away the sins of the world, have mercy upon us.'

What does it mean to say: 'O Lamb of God, that takest away the sins of the world' – to identify Jesus with the Lamb, the traditional sacrificial victim in the Temple worship? What does it mean to see Jesus as the Lamb that God himself provides as he once provided the ram for Abraham's sacrifice in place of Isaac?

Let me tell you what it does *not* mean, for over the centuries there have been some strange and distorting theories about the sacrificial death of Christ. It does not mean that God sent an innocent man to death because he requires blood. The Passion and death of Jesus are not a pagan sacrifice. It does not mean that Jesus came to placate an angry God, nor to show us how we must submit to an inscrutable God – nor did he come to submit himself to a cruel one. Jesus came to do one thing: to embody the love of God for his creation.

Think of the ministry of Jesus: his vision, his compassion, his sacrifice – that is to say, the total giving of himself even unto death – and you see not what God demands of us but what God is prepared to give of himself in order to win us sinners back to him. And not just to win us back in terms of renewing our allegiance to him, but by creating afresh the relationship between him and his creation that human sin has broken – and goes on breaking daily.

And what he does is called 'forgiveness'. In praying that his persecutors may be forgiven, Jesus is looking to the future and absolving his followers of any obligation they might feel to avenge his death. Revenge is no longer an appropriate response. For the old days of an 'an eye for an eye and a tooth for a tooth' are past. The new days of 'forgive and go on forgiving unto seventy times seven' are here. Looking at the cross we are meant to say: 'Look at what we once did to the man who was love incarnate. Look at what we can do to each other by our cruel words and actions. What might we do to change? How shall we act in the light of what we see here?' And it is the people in whom the chain of hurt, resentment and retaliation is broken because their love is not damaged by bitterness or resentment but continues undiminished – it is these people who can truly be said to take away the sins of the world. There is a Jewish saying: 'We must meet extravagant and unreasonable hatred with extravagant and unreasonable love.'

And so we find that at the still centre of the world, at the point where the cross stands, are words of love: 'Father, forgive'. Here is a way of acting that releases love: costly, self-giving love. It's easy to love your friends: we have no problem there. It's possible to feel love for those who suffer, for the poor and the unlovely, and when the world observes such compassion it is moved by it. It's rare to love those who succeed where we fail, to rejoice without envy in the success of those more gifted than we are: rare for the poor to love the rich. The world finds that kind of loving bewildering. But as for the love that forgives the enemy, as for loving the one who mocks and threatens you and inflicts deliberate pain, that is God's love as we see it at Calvary. That love conquers the world. And that is the love God invites us to share.

So what each one of us must ask ourselves on Good Friday is: 'Will I receive that forgiveness?' 'Am I even aware of my need to be forgiven?' There was one group of people whom Jesus could not help: those who did not recognize their own sinfulness, who were too proud or too blind to ask to be forgiven. Or course, most of us are not killers, rapists or pornographers, but only the most unperceptive of us fail to make a connection between the headline violence and the power of evil and what our own sinfulness may do – our own hurt pride, our quickness to take offence, our anger, our lust, our wounding words or loveless actions.

If it is true that God was in Christ, then to preach Christ crucified is to speak in terms that are valid for every generation of the open-hearted love of God that values each of us so highly as to endure the cross for us – and to do it without wanting to make us feel unworthy or guilty but simply forgiven, accepted and loved.

'O Lamb of God, that takest away the sins of the world, have mercy upon us.' Have mercy on us and our own careless, divided hearts. Have mercy on all perpetrators of dreadful deeds and their victims.

Can there be a more hopeful, life-enhancing message than this: that the man on the cross is the embodiment of God's love; that, through an act of sheer, undeserved grace we are reconciled to the God who not only creates us but redeems us, and that out of this terrible death came a new quality of life, a new relationship with all who wish to claim it? And from Calvary the healing power of God still flows within our sick and broken world. That is why, of all the possible words the Church could have used to describe this day of Christ's death, the word they settled on was 'good'.

15

The Way to Which We Are Committed
Good Friday

God was in Christ reconciling the world to himself. 2 Corinthians 5.19

Jesus, whose words were listened to by some with wonder and delight and by others with anger and incomprehension, spoke as much about suffering as about joy. He had told people that when life asks us for more than we can give, or takes from us what we feel we can't spare, that it is only in our giving, in our letting go, that true happiness is to be found. But now they are taking his life. How will he endure? He had spoken of the need to respond to hatred and persecution with forgiveness and love, and to trust the Father whatever may come.

So they watch him, watch him turn to face Jerusalem, watch him cleanse the Temple of the moneychangers, watch his agony in the garden, watch his disciples desert him, watch him stand trial and undergo torture and go to his death. And now they watch him most especially on the cross: a handful who love him, but many more who are indifferent or dismissive.

And what do they see? They see his compassion. As the nails are driven home and soldiers string him up and the crowds mock him, he responds with the words: 'Father, forgive them, for they know not what they do.' And then a little later, they see his apparent dereliction and hear the words: 'My God, my God, why hast thou forsaken me?' For as the darkness deepens he feels that the intimate presence of God with which he has always lived is being withdrawn. And in that cry can be heard every human cry of anguish and loneliness and despair, then and now. To meditate on these words on the cross is to be drawn into the intolerable nature of the world's pain and despair.

Now it is not for a preacher on Good Friday to come up with slick and easy answers to the most profound questions around Easter. Indeed, those who first speak of the death of Jesus in the light of Easter know they are handling events that are ultimately a profound mystery. What the gospel claims is that if we wish to know what our God is like, how he is present in his world, then this is the place to look, the cross. For this man was so open to the Father's love, so uniquely close to the Father's heart, that in St John's words, 'He has made him known.' And so John Austin Baker can write: 'The crucified Jesus is the only accurate picture of God the world has ever seen, and the hands that hold us in existence are pierced with unimaginable nails.'

On the cross we see what it truly means to be human and what it truly means to be God. It means self-giving love. 'The self-giving love of Calvary', wrote Archbishop Michael Ramsey, 'discloses the essence of Godhood in its perfection . . . the glory of God in all eternity is that ceaseless self-giving love of which Calvary is the measure.'

This is how the bridge is built between God and man. This is what we call the atonement – literally, the at-one-ment, the reconciliation: 'God was in Christ reconciling the world to himself' – not by changing his attitude to us but by revealing what it is once and for all in a definitive, unmistakable way. Jesus is for ever the outward and visible sign of what God's love is like.

'And they sat down and watched him there.' When you consider that the first disciples were witnessing the crucifixion, isn't it remarkable that when they looked back at the dreadful things that had happened to their Lord, it made them understand not simply the love of Jesus but the love of God?

Now despite Good Friday, I don't believe we shall ever fully know in this life the answer to the question: 'Why?' 'Why is there undeserved suffering and evil?' But since Good Friday we do know the answer to the question: 'How?' How it can be used and redeemed; for with God on our side, and in the spirit of Jesus, we can take the chaotic, meaningless raw material of suffering, fashion it and make use of it. When suffering comes, you enter a kind of gully of self-pity and despair, yet beyond it there is another country where what is evil may begin to be redeemed.

And those words of desolation, 'My God, my God, why have you forsaken me?' from Psalm 22 are the words of a man trying to make sense of suffering. But while the psalm begins by blaming God, it goes on to a reassertion of faith and the conviction that ultimately the whole world will acknowledge that God is good and to be trusted. And so as Jesus' sense of the goodness of God comes into focus again, he is at last able to give the great shout of triumph: 'It is accomplished!' and to die with his own intimate, affectionate word for God – '*Abba*, Father' – on his lips: 'Father, into thy hands I commend my spirit.' And so the man who has taught them that not a sparrow falls to the ground without the Father's knowledge shows that for him death itself is included in the divine fatherliness, that like every other experience in life it is an opportunity, the final opportunity, to accept in faith that God is to be trusted; that, in the words of Dame Julian of Norwich, 'All shall be well, and all manner of things shall be well.'

As I grow older I believe more and more that this world is a place above all for learning how to love and how to trust. To sit and watch Jesus on his cross, to hear his words and observe the manner of his dying is to see what that loving, trusting relationship with the Father really means. Yet the cross is not just to be looked at. It is to be seized, entered into and made our own. It is stamped on our forehead at baptism: it is the way to which we are committed. And to be a Christian means to belong to the community that tries to live like Jesus, with his kind of loving, his kind of forgiving, his kind of thankfulness and his kind of trust. If we can begin to learn to live like this, if we can meet suffering like this, if in the end we can face our own death like this, then the Spirit of Jesus lives in us and we in him in all the power of his crucified and risen life.

16

The Aching Heart of God
Good Friday

Pilate had an inscription written and nailed to the cross. It read,
'Jesus of Nazareth, the King of the Jews.' John 19.19

A retreat conductor once began an address by pointing to the man hanging on the cross and saying: 'What a way to run a universe!'

I can only account for the hunger of the spirit that I know at my own centre, this muffled yet persistent yearning for God: if it is true that life is the gift of a loving Creator; that I am created by Love to respond with love; that in so doing I shall become what I truly am. Part of my experience bears out that truth and part denies it utterly. For the darkness is too close, the evil too sickeningly real – the Holocaust and the cancer cell, the terrorist bomb and the black depression, the experience of sickness, pain or bereavement that can send you spinning and paralyse you emotionally and spiritually. In the face of such darkness, logic flies out of the window and words become empty, broken things.

There are a thousand sermons to be preached on Good Friday about the mystery of Christ's Passion, but we can only touch the surface of it. Yet I believe this is the absolute heart of it: that if you press more and more deeply into the darkness you will never find a God who answers our bewildered questions but one who enters into them himself – a God who is revealed in the only terms we can understand, as one who shares in the dirt and the pain, the weakness, the loneliness and the dying that we experience ourselves. He asks of us nothing he has not been prepared to share, for the very heart of God is sacrificial love. That is the measure of the mystery and the wonder of Good Friday.

Over the centuries there have been some strange, unappealing theories about the sacrificial death of Christ, seeming to suggest that in his Passion and death Jesus paid the penalty to an angry God who requires his blood. We would be well rid of them. Of course the cross utterly changes our relationship to God, for it changes our whole understanding of his nature, this loving Creator who speaks our language and shares our life. This is how the bridge is built between the Creator and his creatures. We are at one with God again, and so we speak of the at-one-ment, the atonement, the fact that 'God was in Christ reconciling the world to himself.'

'And they sat down and watched him there.' And what do they see? They see his compassion, they hear his words of forgiveness, they witness his apparent desolation as the darkness deepens and he feels that the intimate presence of the Father, which has sustained him through each new day, is being withdrawn. They see a man so at one with every other victim of darkness raging against the dying of the light. As he commends his spirit into his Father's hands, they watch him die. The crowd mocked, the soldiers played their dice and only Mary, John and some of the women kept watch beside him. Nevertheless, when his followers looked back at this terrible, awesome day, it brought them to a new awareness, not simply – as you would expect – of the love and forgiveness of Jesus, but amazingly, and as you would not expect, of the love and forgiveness of God.

'What a way to run a universe!' For a God who is Christlike and whose nature is love, there is no other way possible.

In the end Good Friday is not a day of endless words. It is a day for silence and penitence, a day when we can drop our pretences as we come to kneel at the foot of the cross, admitting the weakness of our faith, our lack of trust, our little love, asking for God's forgiveness and responding to his grace.

Yet the cross is not just to be looked at. It is to be seized, entered into and made our own. To be a Christian is to belong to the community that tries to live like Jesus: with his costly kind of loving and forgiving, his costly kind of daily thankfulness and his costly kind of trust in God, at all times and in all places.

Pilate had an inscription written and nailed to the cross. It read, 'Jesus of Nazareth, the King of the Jews.' And the people mocked him and challenged him, if he was a king, to reign from there. The existence of every church in Christendom, and what God accomplished on Good Friday, is proof that he does.

PART 2

The Seven Last Words of Christ

17

Introduction and First Meditation

For anyone who is in Christ, there is a new creation: the old order is
gone and a new being is there to see. It is all God's word; he reconciled
us to himself through Christ and he gave us the ministry of
reconciliation. 2 Corinthians 5.17-18

My task is clear: to look at the man on the cross, Jesus who was
crucified, yet whom we now honour as Lord and Christ, and to
ask what more we can learn about the mystery of the God who
here stands revealed.

Of all days in the year this is the day for honesty and penitence,
the day when we come face to face with the power of evil and the
nature of our destructive self-centredness. On this day above all
others we see how our deliberately hurtful or simply thoughtless
words and actions may grievously wound us and other people
and the God whose life is within us all. To take Good Friday seriously means we know already at least something of the strange
power of the cross to speak to that restlessness deep within us, a
sense of being incomplete, hungry and thirsty for the God who
is the very source of our life. Nor should we give Good Friday a
second thought if we didn't know our need for forgiveness and
reconciliation.

For most – perhaps all – of us, that sense of dissatisfaction is
experienced chiefly as isolation and as guilt. By isolation I mean
the sense of being alone in a chancy and unpredictable world: of
being unvalued, perhaps unloved and vulnerable, a potential victim of pain, illness, grief and sudden death. By isolation I mean
those times when I look for God but find him strangely silent.
I need the love and reassurance of others, but find if I try to pos-
sess it too greedily it slips from my grasp.

By guilt I simply mean that sense that we are spoiled, that
we are less than we might be, often harbouring resentments we

find it hard to forgive, and not finding it easy to know ourselves forgiven.

I hope, as we watch how Jesus meets his death, we shall see a little more clearly how the cross speaks directly both to our isolation and our guilt. For what it can and should do is to change, utterly and for ever, our concept of God. What we call the Passion of Jesus, all that suffering Jesus embraced when he chose to enter Jerusalem on Palm Sunday, contains two truths that, once you allow them to ferment away in your mind and heart, are nothing short of life-changing. The first truth is about a kind of suffering willingly entered into for the sake of love, and the second is a discovery about the nature, the 'heart' of God. Let me explain what I mean by each as simply as I can.

'A suffering willingly entered into': although Jesus was like us in living in a dangerous world, where suffering in some form comes to most, his suffering was actively chosen – not in some masochistic or perverse spirit but because there was no other way he could act if he was to be true and consistent to all he was and all he had taught. Jesus had one aim, which was to preach the kingdom of God's love and justice, to bring to the sick, the poor, the sinful, the self-righteous, the perplexed, the truth of the Father's compassionate, undiscriminating love: the truth of a new kind of living where you don't dismiss outsiders as worthless, rather you eat with them; where you don't meet hatred or match abuse with resentment or angry retaliation, rather with forgiveness and love. This is not love as a romantic feeling, an emotion, but love that means the deliberate and costly giving of yourself for the good of another who may even be your enemy: giving your time, giving your attention, giving – if need be – your very life itself.

If the first truth learned from Jesus' Passion concerns the costliness of true self-giving love, the 'suffering willingly entered into' for the sake of another, the second truth is that such compassionate love best describes the nature of God. What Good Friday does is to invite us once again to open ourselves to the God who doesn't answer our Job-like questions about the 'Why?' of evil and pain and suffering: instead he enters into the heart of the questions himself. 'The crucified Jesus is the only accurate picture of God the world has ever seen.'

I have sometimes tried to sum up why I am a Christian by saying that it is because I believe in the Passion of Jesus and the compassion of God, and that they alone make sense of life in this world: a world that has pain and suffering deeply ingrained within it, a God whom I learn from the New Testament loves me beyond my imagining, and a bringing of the two together at a place called Calvary, where I can see plainly what that suffering alongside us that is compassion really means and glimpse the mystery of the open-hearted consoling love of God.

The Passion and cross of Jesus are not some momentary 'blip', some fault in the central system where everything suddenly went wrong. They are the single still 'frame', as it were, that reveals how God is and always will be. There can be no more consoling truth than that, nor one that touches our human experience at a deeper level.

And so in the next seven addresses I shall follow the traditional pattern of looking at each of Jesus' words from the cross. But let's be sure we understand what they are, these much-meditated-upon words of Jesus.

No one Gospel writer records all seven: St Mark and St Matthew give only one: the cry of Jesus out of the depth of his forsakenness. St John and St Luke between them give us the other six. We can never know exactly what cries Jesus uttered in those last desperate hours, but that isn't the point. The point is that many years later each Gospel writer was selecting his material in the light of Easter, and in the light of what he *now* knew of the God who had vindicated Jesus by raising him to new life. So what the seven last words from the cross conveyed to them and to the early Church is the truth, the heart, the essence of what Jesus did in his life and the way he faced his death, the essence of what God has achieved in Christ for us. And I shall hope to show once again how these seven words, brought together by the four evangelists, touch on and illuminate every aspect of human life and every experience we may ever be called on to undergo.

18

The First Word

'Father, forgive them, for they know not what they do'

And when they came unto the place which is called The Skull, they crucified him. And Jesus said, 'Father, forgive them, for they know not what they do.' Luke 23.33–34

There is a terrible poignancy and urgency about the last words of those about to die. And it helps us understand the last words of Jesus if we ask: 'Why was he killed?' Was it because the political activists were angry that he hadn't led a popular insurrection against the occupying Roman army? Yes, partly. Was it because the Romans saw him as a threat to peace and security, this so-called King of the Jews? Yes, partly. Was it because the Jewish leaders thought him a dangerous radical who broke the Sabbath, claimed a unique relationship with God and said God was on the side of the poor and marginalized members of society rather than the rich – the sinful rather than the self-righteous? No doubt that, too, threatened them and made them hate him. It was also because he spoke about a kingdom in which all the world's standards are turned on their heads.

So now they stand around and watch him as he meets his death. Will he be true to all he has taught and lived in these last agonizing hours?

What, then, do we see? Helpless, broken in body, Jesus remains consistent, all of a piece. Even in dying he reveals what life in the kingdom means. Where we would rage and hit back, he forgives. He taught his followers to forgive each other and to forgive their enemies as the only effective way of redeeming the past and walking creatively into the future. Now as he is nailed to the cross, the moment when the greatest wrong is done to this good man, he says 'Father, forgive'. And as the Greek words make clear, he doesn't just say it once, he keeps on saying it. 'Father, forgive them, for they know not what they do.' He knows that in God's terms there is no alternative to endlessly repeated forgiveness.

In all his teaching about the Father and our relationship with him and with each other, Jesus had spoken of forgiveness. It's at the heart of a parable like that of the prodigal son, at the heart of such actions as his refusal to condemn the woman taken in adultery – at the heart of the Lord's Prayer: 'When you pray, say "Forgive us our trespasses as we forgive those who trespass against us."' So now, as the nails are driven in, as the crowd taunts him, as one of the thieves curses him, he goes on asking, 'Father, forgive them, they know not what they do.' Like a social worker pleading for a client or a delinquent teenager, he petitions the judge: 'You see, my Lord, he's not fully responsible; he didn't know what he was doing.'

Of course, in one sense they know very well what they do. What they don't know, because they are so blind to the truth not only about him but about themselves, is that they are damaging and twisting their true humanity by acting in this way. All of us are creatures made in God's likeness: made by Love for love. And when we act selfishly, aggressively, lustfully, spitefully, uncharitably, we damage ourselves and stifle that which is of God within us. We are both crucifying God and crucifying our true selves. And the awful thing about retaliating and hitting back, or refusing to forgive a hurt, is that it always adds just a little more poison to the system.

There is only one action that has the necessary power to neutralize the harm and change us at the profoundest level – to accept that we are forgiven ourselves for every fault and then, in our turn, to forgive.

For see what Jesus does. He doesn't say to his followers: 'Forget the cross, forget the Holocaust, forget the murder of Catholic by Protestant and of Protestant by Catholic in Northern Ireland.' He says that only something new and deeply costly has the power to begin to change what is evil. For himself, he looks to the future and absolves his followers from any obligation they might feel to avenge him. For the old days of 'an eye for an eye and a tooth for a tooth' are past. The new days of 'forgive and go on forgiving unto seventy times seven' are here. Looking at the cross we are meant to say: 'Look at what we can do to each other by our cruel words and actions. What might we do to change? How shall we act in the light of what we see here?' And still today it is people in whom the chain of pain, resentment and retaliation is broken because their love is not damaged by bitterness or resentment but continues undiminished – it is these people who can truly be said to take away the sins of the world.

And so in this first word of Jesus we find that at the still centre of the world, at the point where the cross stands, are words of love: 'Father, forgive'. Here is a way of acting that releases love – costly, self-giving love. It's easy to love your friends. It's possible to feel love for those who suffer, for the poor and the unlovely, and when the world observes such compassion it is moved by it. It's rare to love those who succeed where we fail, to rejoice without envy in the success of those more gifted than we are, rare for the poor to love the rich. The world finds that kind of loving bewildering. But as for the love that forgives the enemy, as for love for the one who mocks and threatens you and inflicts deliberate pain, that is God's love as we see it at Calvary. That love conquers the world. And that is the love God invites us to share.

But the questions to each one of us on Good Friday are: 'Will you receive that forgiveness?' 'And will you then, in your turn, forgive?'

I close this meditation with the words of Austin Farrer:

God forgives me with the compassion of his eyes, but my back is turned to him. I have been told that he forgives me, but I will not turn and have the forgiveness, not though I feel the eyes on my back. God forgives me, for he takes my head between his hands and he turns my face to his to make me smile at him. And though I struggle and hurt those hands – for they are human, though divine, human and scarred with nails – though I hurt them, they do not let go until he has smiled me into smiling; and that is the forgiveness of God.

19

The Second Word
'Believe me, today you shall be with me in Paradise'

And he said, 'Jesus, remember me when you come into your kingdom.'
And Jesus said unto him, 'Believe me, today you shall be with me in
Paradise.' Luke 23.42–43

It's been suggested that the penitent thief was perhaps a revolutionary idealist, a man of hope wanting to bring about by violence a different world he passionately wanted to see, who at the last glimpses in this man dying by his side some new truth about who is in the right and who is in the wrong. Perhaps he was a man who in the flame of a shared suffering sees that there is more to living and dying than he had guessed, and that the 'more' has much to do with the man at his side. 'We indeed suffer justly', he says to his fellow-robber; 'This man did nothing wrong.' Somehow, somewhere, the tables may be turned and the victim from Nazareth will be seen to be the victor. And so this man meets his death buoyed up by his new-found hope: 'Jesus, remember me when you come into your kingdom.'

Well, perhaps St Luke wants us to understand something like that. Perhaps he means it to be seen as a genuine act of repentance in the face of death – repentance that means a change of perception, a new attitude, a new way of seeing God and others and ourselves: a new start. So that 'remember me' can be understood not just as 'don't forget me' but the much more positive '*Remember* me: put me – put all my members – together again anew.' Perhaps it was like that.

Or perhaps this is just an example of one *in extremis* clutching at any straw. Yet the response is uncompromising: 'Believe me, today you shall be with me in Paradise.'

This is the word that most powerfully and directly speaks of God's compassion, as that has consistently been revealed in the actions and parables of Jesus. Here, if you like, is the ultimate act of compassion to crown a ministry not just to the sick, the sinful and the poor but to the confused, the anxious, the unvalued and the lost. 'Christ's proper work', wrote Martin Luther, 'is to declare the grace of God, to console and to enliven.' And I do not know which is the more striking fact about the ministry of Jesus: that he cuts through all the religious and social conventions of his time to embrace those who are outsiders in all kinds of senses, or that time and again his encounter is with one insignificant, perfectly ordinary individual like Zacchaeus, the Samaritan woman at the well, a child who is sick or some paralysed, guilty or lost person in need. And in doing so he shows that every one of us is extra-ordinary and of infinite value to God.

Jesus knows the Father as the one who in his parable of the prodigal son waits and watches and cannot contain his joy when his son, whom he has never ceased for an instant to love, returns home, only to find his father running to meet and embrace him. I know, as any counsellor knows, how many of us find it hard to believe we are loved and valued for our own sake, hard to believe that the lover's words to his or her beloved, 'I love you because you are you', are equally the words of God to each last unique one of us, hard to see that Good Friday shows once and for all how God's judgement and God's mercy go hand in hand, and how his judgement is his mercy: 'I love you because you are you.'

And yet it would be dangerous, and do less than justice to our dignity and freedom, to take Jesus' words to the penitent thief as proof that there is no urgency about our encounter with God, that we may just leave things in the hope that we shall get a lucky break on our deathbed like that seventeenth-century epitaph for a man killed by falling from his horse:

Betwixt the stirrup and the ground
Mercy I asked, mercy I found.

For Jesus also told that sharp story of the wise and foolish virgins, and how the latter didn't get into the kingdom because they failed to buy any oil for their lamps. And what I take that story to mean is that although you may repent in an instant, you cannot overnight manufacture the fruits of the Christian life. Either you are in love with God, your husband, wife or partner, or you're not. And if you are it changes you and it changes you over the years pretty profoundly. If we merely want God at the end of our lives, but all we have to offer God is the burnt out fire of our love, we shall still have him. If we invite him he always comes. But it may be that without him we shall have become so self-centred, so full of self that there will be no room for God and no desire for him either. Remember St Augustine's words poured out in distress: 'Too late have I loved ye, O thou beauty of ancient days yet ever new!' When he wrote that he was 32 years old.

I used to believe that God's love is quite simply unconditional. But now I see there is a sense in which that isn't so. God's love is uncalculating and never withdrawn, but if we are to experience it, there is a condition, and that is that we want it and make some effort to respond to it. If my wife loves me but I pay her no attention and behave towards her thoughtlessly and make no effort to love her in return, you cannot say I experience love in the full meaning of the word. So with God. I can't experience his love whatever I do. For his love is like the wind, but it only blows in one direction, towards fuller and deeper life and fulfilment for me and for all the world. If I go in some other direction I shall find that wind of the spirit of life in differing degrees against me, blowing in my face, not at my back. The Bible is so sure of this that it says we can only then know his love for us as wrath.

So we find in this promise of Paradise, this promise of Jesus to the thief that he will be with Christ through and beyond his death, a consistent compassion and the assurance that at the moment we really want God then we have him. Yet we must balance the drama of a deathbed conversion against everything we know of what it can mean to grow within the relationship of giving and receiving love. The life into which Christ invites us is one in which he has said: 'Behold, I am with you always', and of which we can say in the now that is today: 'I believe that you are with me, in every moment of my life, both here and hereafter.'

20

The Third Word
'Woman, behold your son'

When Jesus saw his mother, and the disciple whom he loved standing
near, he said to his mother, 'Woman, behold your son!' John 19.26

Does our Creator weep? The crucified child of Mary, the Son of
God, is the Father's answer.

Consider Mary and the cost to her as she watches this man die
in agony. This is the one who as an infant she has carried in her
womb – whom as a child she has taught to speak and to whom
as a growing adult she has taught those truths that lie closest to
her heart.

For she has taught him – the one who is in the world to reveal
the Father's will and the Father's love – what it means to love
and be loved, taught him what it means to do the Father's will.
She has taught him how to move from the utter dependence of
the child to the independence of the man. Taught him how to
face life with spontaneity and courage. Mary taught him all she
knew – and then let him go.

But it is not simply the self-giving quality of love that Jesus
has learned from Mary, but also what it means to do the will of
God. Mary's response at the annunciation had been: 'Be it unto
me according to thy word.' She was ready for whatever joy and
whatever pain this burden might bring, prepared for the piercing
of her heart. Here is what is required of us: an attitude, an open-
ness to life and to the utterly trustworthy and caring God who
is at the heart of it. Jesus shared that attitude of trust, though at
great cost, and what the agony in the Garden is about is saying
in the face of great suffering and certain death: 'be it unto me

according to thy word' in the spirit of trust he had first learned at his mother's knee.

'Woman', Jesus had said to his mother at the wedding in Cana of Galilee, 'my hour is not yet come.' Now it has come, and again he uses the deliberately formal word 'Woman'. 'Woman, behold your son; son, behold your mother.' From a very early date Christians have seen that action as far more than a loving concern of this son for this mother. It has been understood at many levels. Mary and John are given to each other in a new reality of love that is the beginning of God's new creation. Each has loved him deeply. Each must now let him go, for each is now to discover him alive again in the other. Further, Christians have seen the beloved disciple as here representing every Christian, and Mary the mother as Mother Church – that is to say, here is the icon, the kernel of the new community that is to be born out of the experience of Good Friday and Easter. It is from this experience of death and resurrection that the Church, by its teaching, fellowship, sacrament and prayer, creates and nurtures all who recognize the authority of Jesus Christ and become part of the new Christian family. This new community is symbolized by Mary and John – maturity and youth, female and male, the old tradition and the new adventure of faith in Jesus, all one now in Christ. Here at the foot of the cross, in the person of his mother and the beloved disciple, is the point of pain and love where the Church is born. Its task will be to teach its members what it means to love and be loved. It is to teach us too what it may mean to say in trust, in all life's unpredictability: 'Be it unto me according to thy word.'

And so what Jesus has first begun to learn within the circle of a girl's arms – the meaning of the give and take of love and the meaning of trust, come what may – must now be learned by every Christian within the community in which he or she is baptized. So much I dare to think lies contained within what St John would have us understand by the words: 'Woman, behold thy son; son, behold thy mother.'

21

The Fourth Word
'My God, my God, why have you forsaken me?'

And Jesus cried in a loud voice: 'My God, my God, why have you
forsaken me?' Matthew 27.46; Mark 15.34

These words were found written on the wall of a cellar in which
a Jewish victim of the Holocaust hid and died:

I believe in the sun even when it is not shining.
I believe in love where feeling is not.
I believe in God even if he is silent.

If it is true that 'all that matters is to be at one with the living
God' (D. H. Lawrence, 'Pax'), then there is no worse evil that
can befall us than to die rejected by men and apparently aban-
doned by God – a cursed blasphemer, tortured, spat upon and
jeered at, and left to die on the rubbish heap outside the city
wall. Jesus on the cross experiences the extreme limit of alienation and darkness. Like all of us, he was fearful of death and
the process of dying. Now the darkness deepens and his sense of
God vanishes – has he perhaps been wrong all the time? Now he
too begins to 'rage, rage, against the dying of the light' (Dylan
Thomas, 'Do not go gentle into that good night').

In his extremity of desolation Jesus is using that richest of
all treasuries for every human experience, the psalms – in this
case, Psalm 22. And it's often pointed out that this psalm, which
begins with the cry of deep distress, 'My God, my God, why have
you forsaken me?', moves through marked changes of mood,
all the way from blaming God to a final reassertion of faith and

the certainty that deliverance will come: the conviction that ultimately the whole world will acknowledge God's goodness.

Now what does it mean to work through a time of great suffering? It means you must resist in the deepest part of your being the contracting of your whole world into a single blinding point of pain. It means a great act of will so that you may recover your sense of the reality of God and your belief that in the end, to quote Dame Julian of Norwich, 'All shall be well . . . and all manner of thing shall be well.'

Yet I want to stay for the moment with the anguish and the desolation as yet unresolved, because it seems to me to be at this point that the nature of the God incarnate in this man Jesus is most sharply seen. Here is mystery indeed. Here in this dark hour is the divine pity revealed, God at one with all who, for whatever reason, feel they are forsaken.

I find this anguished cry of Jesus of such great comfort because in it I hear the cry of all in our time who experience total darkness and alienation. Here the Passion of Jesus links with the Passion of all men and women. The stories, the diaries and letters and poems of our time record many journeys that end in violent death – many hopes turned to dust and ashes. Surely the most potent figure of our time is the Jewish refugee whose journey ended not in the Promised Land but in the gas chambers along with eight million of his or her fellow human beings. There are a few places the whole world knows: Golgotha, Belsen, Ravensbrück and Auschwitz: the old prison camps of Siberia, the Cambodia of Pol Pot, the Uganda of Idi Amin and a thousand places where men and women, made like us in God's image and each of infinite and unique worth, are abused, tortured so that they may betray their friends, imprisoned for conscience's sake and killed.

Yes, the Passion goes on. And here is the strangest paradox and to our minds the deepest mystery: that the crucified Jesus, who at this point knew to the full the ultimate isolation of the human spirit apparently cut off from God, is at the same time 'the only accurate picture of God the world has ever seen'. If we believe that God is reconciling the world to himself by revealing his 'human face' in Jesus, then we must be willing to have our understanding of God profoundly changed. Here is a God who shares the dirt and the pain, the weakness and the loneliness, the very death that we experience ourselves.

Every year on Good Friday people die, and some at least will, in their time of suffering, feel forsaken by God, afraid of the dark and cheated of life. I remember some words of Dame Cicely Saunders, one of the founders of the Hospice Movement, saying once in my church out of the depth of her long experience with the suffering and the dying:

> Surely all the hard things that have happened to anyone in his creation have happened to God himself. As any mother, seeing her child suffer, is suffering herself, so the Father of everyone has received all the sorrow and pain himself . . . and the presence of Jesus in history was the presence of God as he has always been and will always be.

Like any priest I have celebrated both the joys and the sorrows of human life. In terms of the latter I have sat with the dying, tried to console the bereaved, spent hour upon hour encouraging the unloved and listening to the wounded and the lonely. I have also known the dereliction of a long, debilitating illness, when it was almost impossible to pray at all. And all I know is that, for me, the only words that have helped have had to do with Christ crucified: or rather, the Easter Christ who still bears in his hands the marks of the nails and the wound in his side. The only words that I sense have helped others have had to do with the concept of the suffering God, whose love for each of us cannot be altered or diminished and of whom I can say with the psalmist: 'If I reach up to heaven, thou art there: if I go down to hell thou art there also.'

I began with those words scratched on the wall of a concentration camp prison:

> I believe in the sun even when it is not shining.
> I believe in love where feeling is not.
> I believe in God even if he is silent.

What the cry of desolation of Jesus the crucified reveals is the God who is with us at the most desperate point of human need.

22

The Fifth Word
'I thirst'

After this, Jesus, aware that all had now come to its appointed end,
said, 'I thirst.' John 19.28

The centre of me is always and eternally a terrible pain. A curi-
ous wild pain – a searching for something beyond what the
world contains, something transfigured and infinite – the beauti-
ful vision – God. I do not find it, I do not think it is to be found –
but the love of it is my life. It's the passionate love for a ghost.

The moving words of an unbeliever, the great philosopher
Bertrand Russell. And they speak of a kind of wanting, a thirst,
a sense of incompleteness within us all, believer and unbeliever
alike. We may be dust, but we are dust that dreams of a glory
in store for us. This yearning, this need to look beyond myself,
this desire to know myself accepted, loved and valued, which we
know best perhaps in moments of stillness, moments when we
are giving attention – this wanting is a thirst for God. Nothing
less than God can satisfy us. Nothing less than God himself can
ultimately give significance to our lives or any real meaning to
our experience of loss, suffering and death.

And when St John records that Jesus at the end says, 'I thirst',
he wants us to understand in the most profound way that Jesus
is expressing that consuming thirst for God that burns beneath
all he said or did. His whole life had been a desire to do the will
of God: 'Not my will, but thine, be done.'

Now St John, in composing his Gospel, does nothing without a purpose. He tells us that when Jesus was handed over for
crucifixion 'it was about the sixth hour', in the full heat of the

day. In fact he has used that phrase once before near the start of his story and expects us to catch the echo. He tells us, in chapter four, that 'it was about the sixth hour' when Jesus comes to Jacob's well and is thirsty, and says to the Samaritan woman: 'Give me a drink.' That famous well, dug by Jacob, is 75 feet deep, and at the bottom of it stands a spring of water that is still bubbling and flowing today, a life-giving oasis in the arid desert. What follows, in the encounter with the Samaritan woman and her reluctance to have any dealings with a Jewish man, is the revelation that Jesus himself can offer 'living' water; indeed, that he is himself the 'living' water – water that is alive with a new quality of life. In St John's mind Jacob's well stands for the old order, a symbol of God's dealing with Israel through Abraham, Moses and Jacob. Now the new order, the new creation, is to begin with the giving of the Holy Spirit and a whole new understanding of the God of love spelled out in the life, death and resurrection of Jesus Christ. 'Everyone who drinks of this well-water', Jesus tells the woman, 'will thirst again' – that is to say, the water of the old order, the old religion, will only satisfy for a while. 'But no one who drinks the water that I shall give him will ever be thirsty again: the water that I shall give him will become in him a spring of water, welling up for eternal life.'

And now the one who claims to give this living water that will satisfy our deepest need, which is our need of God, says, as he said to the woman by the well, 'I thirst.' With every last breath in his body he thirsts and longs for God, just as throughout his life he has longed to open blind eyes and unstop deaf ears in showing men and women what God is truly like, and pointing them to the one who alone can give their lives a meaning and a purpose.

But the world stays true to itself and offers him sour wine. A soldier holds up his spear and offers him vinegar on a sponge.

'I thirst.' While it has for St John a profound symbolic significance, it is also the simple expression of the most basic need. You can live for a good while without food; you cannot long survive without water. So consider how the tables have been turned for Jesus, as they are turned for us all eventually as we move through our lives from a state of vigorous activity to a state of passive dependence on others. Jesus, the dynamic, active teacher and itinerant preacher, is reduced to a silent, passive man, at the mercy of those around him. Now he is helpless, unable to move, as dependent on the kindness, the indifference or the brutality of others as are the ill, the old and the disabled of every age.

For Jesus the turning point is Gethsemane, where Judas hands him over to the forces beyond his control. Now his hands are tied, now he is at the disposal of others, the one who patiently endures – not the one who *does* but the one who is *done to*. On the way to Golgotha he cannot even carry his own cross but is waited on, served, by a stranger who happens to be passing by.

There is a fine book by an English theologian, W. H. Vanstone, called *The Stature of Waiting*, in which he relates the active and passive aspects of Jesus' life to the pattern of our own. As we grow older, or if we are disabled, we become those for whom things are done or to whom they are done, and there is a great art in learning how to receive, how to endure patiently and creatively, how to rise to the stature of waiting. For God himself, incarnate in Jesus, has become one who discloses himself to us as a passive receiver and has placed himself wholly in our hands.

And God is to be seen in us both in our active, creative lives and in our passivity when that is forced on us, and he will be seen in the spirit in which we accept what others do for us, in how we respond to those on whom we now depend. Those forced to be inactive or to suffer by sickness, handicap or old age must not feel, and must not be made to feel, that they are any less valuable as human beings, or that they do not have a real contribution to make.

'I thirst.' Nowhere is Jesus more powerful than in his passive suffering on the cross. Nowhere does he show more clearly the truth of the passive, suffering God whose hands are tied by love. Like each word from the cross, here are layers of meaning that I can do no more than hint at. Here, in these words, 'I thirst', is an expression of the deepest human need for God. Here is an ironic echo of the words at Jacob's well, for this man – through his Passion and resurrection and the giving of the Spirit – will indeed become the living water flowing within us. And here, incredibly, is God, as nakedly vulnerable as is any dying man, parched with thirst and pleading for a cup of water.

23

The Sixth Word
'It is accomplished'

Having received the vinegar Jesus said: 'It is accomplished!' John 19.30

We have been considering the mystery at the heart of what we call the Incarnation, of a man so open to God, so at one with his will at every point of his life, so close to the Father's heart, that when we look at him we see God. It isn't that Jesus is just like God, for who can conceive what God is like in all his mysterious, transcendent power, the one to whom we cry 'Holy, holy, holy, Lord God of hosts: heaven and earth are full of your glory?' Rather, it is that the one we call God, the one who is the very ground of our being, is Christlike. In Archbishop Michael Ramsey's fine phrase: 'God is Christlike, and in him is no unChristlikeness at all.' The loving, forgiving, compassionate, affirming, foot-washing, self-sacrificing Jesus Christ reveals the essence of all we need to know of God in the only terms we can understand: in human terms, speaking our language, part of our world.

God is with us, on our side. God is not the one who requires the suffering and death of Jesus as a punishment for sin, as some of those terrible medieval theories of what we call the atonement suggest. God – and there is no greater mystery than this – is the one who suffers and dies in Jesus and who himself experiences all our bewildered agony where all our questions hang and no explanation satisfies. He doesn't answer those questions. Somehow, in the Word made flesh, he enters into the heart of them himself. On the cross we see what it truly means to be human and what it truly means to be God: it means self-giving love. 'The self-giving love of Calvary', wrote Archbishop Michael Ramsey, 'discloses the essence of deity in its perfection . . . the glory of God in all eternity is that ceaseless self-giving love of which Calvary is the measure.'

And this is how the bridge is built between God and man. This is what we call the atonement – literally the at-one-ment, the reconciliation: 'God was in Christ reconciling the world to himself' – not by changing God's attitude to his creatures but by revealing it once and for all in a definitive way. Jesus is for ever the outward and visible sign of what God's love is like.

So the cross shows us the ultimate logic of our sin, self-centredness, wilful blindness and our little love: what it does to us and what it does to God. And the cross shows us the invincible love of God. The kind of love that comes closest, I suppose, is that of a mother for her child whatever he or she may do.

There's a medieval poem that goes like this:

A poor lad once and a lad so trim,
Gave his heart to her who loved not him;
And said she 'Bring me tonight, you rogue,
Your mother's heart to feed my dog.'

To his mother's house went the young man,
Killed her, cut out her heart, and ran.
But as he was running, look you, he fell,
And the heart rolled out on the ground as well.

And the lad, as the heart was a-rolling, heard
The heart was speaking and this was the word –
The heart was a-weeping, and crying so small:
'Are you hurt, my child? Are you hurt at all?'

It doesn't matter what you do to a mother's love, her sole concern is what has happened to you in the process. Are you hurt? It doesn't matter what you do to God: ignore him, say he doesn't exist, crucify him – his one concern is the hurt you do to yourself. When you consider that the first disciples were witnesses of the crucifixion, isn't it remarkable that when they looked back at the dreadful things that had happened to their Lord it made them understand not simply the love of Jesus but the love of God?

So the at-one-ment between God and mankind means we are brought into a new relationship with each other, one requiring real change, so that our lives take on both a new dimension and a new direction. And what the cross says to me is not that God will forgive me if I repent and mend my ways, but much more important, that God without waiting for me to repent has wrought an act of reconciliation that at once changes everything.

There is a feeble gospel and there is a powerful gospel. The feeble gospel sees Jesus as our pattern, our example. Such a gospel may not do much harm but it has no power to change our lives. It leaves you untouched at the centre. But the powerful gospel has at its heart the cross and Passion of Jesus, the compassion of God. It speaks of forgiveness, of death and of new life. The feeble gospel says, 'You may be forgiven'; the powerful gospel says, 'You are redeemed!' And properly to understand the powerful gospel, that of the cross and the resurrection, is to be seized by the vision of a world turned topsy-turvy: a world in which greatness means the service of others and love means the giving of yourself; in which the good will be crucified and glory lies in suffering; in which finding your life means losing it; in which, when judgement and compassion conflict, compassion always wins; in which forgiveness always, in all ways, has the final word.

'It is accomplished!' Jesus has achieved all he came to do. And yet in a sense it is not yet finished. For when we speak of the cross we don't simply mean the suffering of Jesus. We use the word as a kind of shorthand by which we mean God's love declaring itself through this completely offered man, through his whole life, death and resurrection and what follows. For what then follows is the eager and loving response of men and women ever since. The fulfilment of Christ's life and death comes through people identifying themselves with him, living in and by his Spirit, offering themselves to God in trust and becoming open to life. And this must go on until the end of time.

'It is accomplished!' We mustn't forget that St John is writing all this not just in the light of Easter but as one who for much of his life has lived and worshipped in the Church born of the resurrection, and there is in this penultimate word a real sense of victory – a foretaste of Easter. The seven words from the cross between them speak both of desolation and of glory: St Mark and St Matthew focus on the agony but St John tells the story with a title above and beneath and wrapped all about it, and that title is the word 'glory'. The way Jesus meets his death, with trust and with forgiveness on his lips, is his final act of self-giving love, and that is the very glory of the being of God himself.

So Good Friday is a victory. Easter confirms it but it doesn't make it one, for it is a victory already. What Easter does is to bring its power into human lives in any age for those who live in the Spirit of the risen Christ.

'It is accomplished!' When they nailed Jesus to the cross they placed above his head a placard to make the people smirk – Jesus of Nazareth, the King of the Jews. And they said, 'Let him reign from there!'

'Let him reign from there.' The existence of your Church and my church and every church in Christendom, and the witness of the whole company of saints and martyrs, known and unknown, and the witness of countless Christians who in times of suffering and anguish have continued to put their trust in God, prove that he does.

24

The Seventh Word
'Father, into your hands I entrust my spirit'

And when Jesus had cried with a loud voice, he said,
'Father, into your hands I entrust my spirit.' Luke 23.46

The Christian life is about learning how to live here and now in
freedom from fear and self-concern, in trust and love. Indeed, it
might be said that the world is a place where we are to learn to
do two things well: to be thankful at all times and in all places,
and to trust God come what may. To sit and watch Jesus on his
cross, to hear these seven words and observe the manner of his
dying, is to see just what that thankful, trusting relationship with
the Father is to mean.

The crucifixion begins and ends with the same word: Father.
'Father, forgive them'; 'Father, into your hands I entrust my
spirit' – 'Father, *Abba*', the word Jesus has made peculiarly his
own. It's not a formal word, *Abba*, it's the equivalent of our
word 'Dad' or 'Daddy.' The Gospels always use this particular
word when it is on Jesus' lips, both in Aramaic and in Greek.
And I think there can only be one reason for this: that it was a
well-known idiosyncrasy of Jesus when speaking of God to use
this word by which a Jewish child addressed his or her parent. In
so doing he expresses a relationship of extra-ordinary directness
and intimacy.

It is the view of Jesus that everything we experience is undergirded by love. He never claimed that God would protect us
from the violence of life – indeed, quite the contrary. Those who
witness to what is true, good, just and honest may well be called
to suffer, even to die, as Jesus was. What he did say is that 'Not
a sparrow falls to the ground without your Father knowing.' He
saw every natural event as within the purpose and caring of God,

and for Jesus death is included in God's fatherliness. Like every other human experience, it is an occasion for trust.

So it is the word *Abba* that sets the seal of Jesus' life, as it is the Our Father that is the basic Christian prayer. For the Christian, all our questioning of life arises within the context of God's loving care, not the belief that we shall be protected as others aren't. I may lose my child from leukaemia; I may be mugged on the city streets; and it is certain I shall one day die. But we can now say with far greater reason than Job had, 'Though he slay me yet will I trust him': 'underneath are the everlasting arms'.

'Father, into your hands I entrust my spirit.' For Jesus death itself and all the suffering he has endured is included in the divine fatherliness and is an occasion for giving to God until we have nothing more to give. The words he uses come from Psalm 31. They were no doubt taught him by his mother, for it was the verse from the Jewish prayer book that you were to say last thing at night before falling asleep. 'Father, into your hands I entrust my spirit.' It is the simplest, most childlike form of trust.

Jesus had often spoken of the only true way to life: the way of letting go of all that claims us, of dying daily in small ways. For when we come to die finally, we can't hold on to anything – not our families and friends, not our position and possessions, not our power to do good or evil. All has to go. In this way our physical death becomes a kind of parable of how to live the whole of life – letting go, letting God take over, learning to enter the kingdom with open hands like a child receiving gifts.

In the end, the cross is not just to be looked at. It is to be claimed, entered into and made our own. It is placed on our forehead when we are baptized. To be a Christian means to belong to the community that tries to live like Jesus – with his kind of selfless love, his kind of thankfulness, his kind of trust in the undergirding goodness of God. It is a pattern of which we are reminded every Eucharist as we take, give thanks for, break and share the bread that is his body and our own: we in him and he in us.

If we can even a little learn to live like this, meet suffering like this, even in the end die like this, then our Lord Jesus Christ does indeed live in us and we in him, in all the power of his crucified and risen life.

Scripture Index